The English Mystical Tradition

THE ENGLISH MYSTICAL TRADITION

DAVID KNOWLES

Harper & Brothers, New York

NIHIL OBSTAT: JOANNES M. T. BARTON, S.T.D., L.S.S.
CENSOR DEPUTATUS
IMPRIMATUR: ✠ GEORGIUS L. CRAVEN
VICARIUS GENERALIS
EPISCOPUS SEBASTOPOLIS
WESTMONASTERII: DIE XVIII AUGUSTI MCMLX

The Nihil obstat and Imprimatur are a declaration that a book or pamphlet is
considered to be free from doctrinal or moral error. It is not implied that those who
have granted the Nihil obstat and Imprimatur agree with the contents, opinions or
statements expressed.

THE ENGLISH MYSTICAL TRADITION

FIRST EDITION

Library of Congress catalog card number: 61-7343

CONTENTS

CONTENTS

PREFACE

THIS volume incorporates the substance of the *Sir D. Owen Evans Lectures* delivered at the University College of Wales, Aberystwyth, during the Session 1959 to 1960. Those lectures are by their deed of foundation intended to be concerned with the exposition of some aspect of the Christian religion, and I welcomed the opportunity to return to a subject on which I had written a small book many years before. That book, *The English Mystics* (1928), had long been out of print; it was defective in many ways, and besides its intrinsic defects it had, like all other writings on the subject of that date, completely mistaken the significance of Margery Kempe, who was then an unknown and dateless figure prior to the discovery of her *Book* in 1934.

The present work has only a few sentences and quotations in common with its predecessor. In content, the four great mystical writers of the fourteenth century and the post-Reformation Benedictine, Father Augustine Baker, appear in this, as in the previous, book, but whereas a chapter is now devoted to Margery Kempe, that on the *Ancren Riwle* has no counterpart here. In part, this was because the *Ancren Riwle* is not in any real sense of the term a *mystical* book, and partly because it belongs to a large family of treatises on the life of recluses which have become the centre of a whole literature of learned studies in which historians and philologists have been, and are still, deeply engaged, and in which the final reckoning has yet to be made.

As regards method, this book differs from its predecessor in giving more emphasis to the doctrines of the writers concerned. The mystics, in other words, are considered primarily as mystics, and only secondarily as personalities or literary figures. On the personal and philological aspects of their writings much careful scholarship has been expended by a series of the ablest students of Middle English literature, but hitherto, save for the notable work of Father Molinari, S.J., on Julian of Norwich, the doctrinal and ascetical side of the English mystics has been left for treatment to those who have prepared editions of their works for the devout reader. Here, therefore, an attempt has been made to estimate their place in the long history of Catholic spirituality, and their value as guides for readers of the present day.

Besides the authorities of the University College of Wales, Aberystwyth, and all those who made my visit there memorable by their kindly hospitality, I have to thank Sister Anna Maria Reynolds, C.P., and Miss Joy Russell Smith for help in regard to Dame Julian and Walter Hilton, and the late Abbot Justin McCann, O.S.B., for many letters and discussions concerning Father Augustine Baker. Finally, my thanks are due to the Revv. Editors of *The Clergy Review* for permission to use some pages of an article on Fr Baker which appeared in that journal in November, 1958.

DAVID KNOWLES.

Peterhouse,
Cambridge.
13 *June,* 1960.

Chapter I

CHRISTIAN MYSTICISM

THE principal theme of this book will be the English medieval mystics. This title has become conventional for a group of four writers and their less important satellites who flourished between 1330 and 1400: they are, in order of chronology, Richard Rolle, the unknown author of *The Cloud of Unknowing*, Walter Hilton, and Julian of Norwich. In addition, there are the unknown authors of a few minor but similar writings, and the slightly later and, if the phrase be permitted, the less highly respectable Margery Kempe. Taken as a group, with their various gifts and characteristics, they have no parallel in fourteenth-century Europe, and as individuals they are equalled or surpassed only by their eminent contemporaries in Germany, Italy and Flanders, such as Eckhardt (d. 1327), Tauler (d. 1361), Suso (d. 1366), Ruysbroeck (d. 1381) and Catherine of Siena (d. 1380). These names will have served as a reminder that the fourteenth century was peculiarly rich in mystical writers; indeed, it has no rival in all the Christian centuries save the sixteenth century, the age of St Teresa and St John of the Cross. I shall return later to the historical setting of the times, but before embarking upon such a review, it is necessary to define, once for all, our elusive subject.

The word "mystic" and its derivatives, like the almost synonymous word "contemplative", has become in recent times both very popular and extremely ambiguous. To discuss it at length would be impossible here; it must suffice to say that in what follows the words "mystic" and "mystical" will be understood in the sense that was standard among all theologians and religious writers from the early middle ages to the sixteenth century, and which derived its currency from the title of the short treatise by the pseudo-Denis, which he entitled *Theologia Mystica*. Literally this means the secret knowledge of God, and it was translated by one of our English mystics as *Denis Hid Divinity*, which is accurate enough. Mystical theology is thus distinguished both from what is called natural theology and from dogmatic and speculative theology. If by theology we mean the knowledge of God and His ways, it has always been the Christian teaching that we can have knowledge of God as our Maker and Governor by a natural process of reasoning; this is natural theology. To this we add what Jew and Christian have learnt from God's own revelation of Himself through the inspired writers of Scripture, and above all from the words and works of His Son, Jesus Christ. Both these kinds of knowledge are available, so far as the words go, to all men who meet with Christians and their books, but it has always been held that the second kind, God's revelation, can only become real and living by the grace of God and through the gift of faith. Without this gift a Voltaire or a Marx could, by reading and careful expression, give an accurate account of the Christian doctrine of the Trinity, but he could not believe in the truth of that doctrine.

Beyond these kinds of knowledge there is a third by which God and the truths of Christianity can not only be believed and acted upon, but can in varying degrees be directly known and experienced. Such at least is the traditional teaching of the Church, reinforced by the express declarations of theologians and saintly Christians throughout the centuries from the days of the apostles to our own time. This knowledge, this experience, which is never entirely separable from an equally immediate and experimental union with God by love, has three main characteristics. It is recognized by the person concerned as something utterly different from and more real and adequate than all his previous knowledge and love of God. It is experienced as something at once immanent and received, something moving and filling the powers of the mind and soul. It is felt as taking place at a deeper level of the personality and soul than that on which the normal processes of thought and will take place, and the mystic is aware, both in himself and in others, of the soul, its qualities and of the divine presence and action within it, as something wholly distinct from the reasoning mind with its powers. Finally, this experience is wholly incommunicable, save as a bare statement, and in this respect all the utterances of the mystics are entirely inadequate as representations of the mystical experience, but it brings absolute certainty to the mind of the recipient. This is the traditional mystical theology, the mystical knowledge of God, in its purest form.

We have said that this is the traditional teaching of the Church. This is not to imply that at all times the technique of mystical theology has been part of the normal and universal teaching of Christianity, but that at all periods there have been Christians who have experienced this form of communion with God and that from early times and in every age a succession of eminent and saintly persons have given an account of their experiences and that gradually a technical theological description and explanation has grown up. In these pages, it need hardly be said, the Christian position is assumed throughout, and with it an acceptance of the general authenticity and authority of the Scriptures. Without some frame of reference any discussion of the mystical life becomes vague and futile, and my framework is that of a Catholic Christian. It is no part of our task to discuss the possibility of a mystical knowledge of God, nor to decide what relationship, if any, exists between Christian mysticism and apparently similar experiences outside the Church. The English mystics, all of them, were devout and orthodox Catholic Christians, and it is with them that we are dealing. They will be considered in the light of the faith that we share with them.

We may begin, therefore, by recalling the words of Our Lord in the last chapters of St John's gospel, which to us, as to the mystics, are the utterance of Jesus Himself, and which would be accepted even by extreme critics as representing the belief of early Christians. "He who loveth me shall be loved of my Father; and I will love him and make myself manifest to him. . . . If anyone love me he will keep my word. And my Father will love him: and we will come to him and make our abode with him."[1] And again, "I pray that those who shall believe in me may be one, as thou, Father, art in me and I in thee, that they also may be one in us . . . and I have given them the glory which thou hast given me that they may be one as we also are one. I in them and thou in me, that they may be made perfect into one."[2] And the evangelist, writing almost a lifetime after these words were spoken, could write of himself: "We have seen his glory, the glory as of the only begotten of the Father, full of grace and truth."[3] Many Christians, perhaps most of us at one time or another, will have read those words and applied them to what may be called the barest minimum of Christian unity and goodwill, and perhaps to the beginning of divine sonship given at baptism or realized more clearly when we first turned to Christ. But if we are truly Christians, do we really and sincerely think that Our Lord's words mean no more than that, or that they are merely a sublime utterance which has no immediate meaning for Christians here below? Should we not rather, if we believe that these words are the words of God, consider that their true meaning is the literal one, taken in the most sublime sense of which they are susceptible, and

[1] John xiv 21, 23.   [2] *Ibid.*, xvii 21–23.   [3] *Ibid.*, i 14.

that the weak, conventional sense in which we normally understand them is but the palest glimmer of their meaning? Whatever is received, so ran the scholastic axiom, is received according to the capacity of the receiver. Those who best knew the mind of Christ took the words at full strength. When St John the Apostle wrote that the Father hath so loved us that we may be called, and be indeed, the children of God,[4] and St Paul could write of himself "I live now, not I but Christ liveth in me"[5] we cannot be satisfied with understanding the words as merely a *façon de parler* or a surge of emotion. It was the same St Paul who wrote of himself that he had been rapt to paradise and had heard words ineffable, which it was not lawful for a man to utter. Can we doubt that this incommunicable knowledge lay behind those passages in Ephesians and Colossians where the language in which the apostle speaks of Christ touches at once a depth and a simplicity which, we feel, cannot but be an attempt to put into human words a supernatural vision of reality? And from St Paul we may follow the thread through the Alexandrian and Greek Fathers to St Augustine and St Gregory the Great.

How then, have the theologians interpreted the message of the Scriptures? They have taken their stand upon two basic Christian doctrines: the transcendent immanence of God and the divine sonship given us by Christ.

God is at once transcendent and immanent in His creatures. He is transcendent, and therefore cannot be attained or comprehended or experienced as He is in Himself by any created faculty; yet He is immanent in creation by His power, His presence, and His essence, for without this power and presence no creature could exist. This is true of all creation, but it is eminently true of the spiritual world of soul. God is Spirit, and the soul was made in His likeness, with the

---

[4] I John iii 1.   [5] Galat. ii 20.

faculties of knowledge and love and (within limits) of self-determination. God, also, is spirit, truth and love present in the centre of the soul, concealed only by sin and by the finite, human mode of the soul's knowledge and love.

The second great theological principle is that Christ in redeeming mankind gave to man the possibility of sharing in the divine life. "As many as received him, to them he gave power to be made the sons of God."[6] There are many passages in the gospels where Christ Himself makes the same assertion, and once again, when we remind ourselves who is speaking, we shall take due care not to falsify or bowdlerize the words. They fully justify the assertion in the second epistle of St Peter, that Christians are sharers in the divine nature.[7]

All Christians therefore have in germ and may have in flower and fruit, a new, supernatural life. But while we may interpret these phrases in their fullest and most literal sense, remembering whose is the voice and the Spirit within them, we must also remember that, in the words of the evangelist, He giveth grace for grace;[8] that there is no flat rate of grace, that unto one a single talent is given and unto another ten, and that no one cometh to Christ unless the Father draw him. The new life is the free gift of God; it is what we call the life of grace, and God is completely free to give to whom He will, when He wills and in what measure He wills. To every one who is drawn by the Father and does not fail He gives faith and love, invisible, intangible, but real, by which to believe in and to love Him whom we have not seen. We follow the Spirit which blows we know not whence and goes we know not whither. We have no direct experience of grace; our mind and our will, to all appearances, follow their natural way of acting. In theological language the grace, which was freely given to us without merit or effort, now

---

[6] John i 12.   [7] 2 Peter i 4.   [8] John i 16.

co-operates with us in our thoughts and actions which still follow their natural, human way of acting. But among Christians, as among all God's creatures, there is a diversity of gifts, but one Lord. Star differeth from star in glory.[9] Just as among men there are many soldiers and poets and musicians, but only a rare Napoleon or Shakespeare or Mozart, so among Christians there are those to whom a higher knowledge and love are given, and they are by no means always the great bishops and pastors and divines, though among these also there are prophets. These chosen ones are capable of receiving not only the gift of faith and the power to love and serve God, but a new supernatural knowledge and love, the beginnings of God's own knowledge of Himself and love of Himself which is the life of the Blessed Trinity and of the blessed in heaven, who see God as He is and know even as they are known. In them grace does more than co-operate with their human efforts; it operates itself directly in the powers which receive with free consent. Tradition has always attributed this grace to a special gift of the Holy Spirit, and from the age of the Fathers has seen in the seven spirits of Isaiah—fear of God, piety, knowledge, fortitude, counsel, understanding and wisdom—an adumbration of the special Gifts of the Holy Ghost which raise the Christian life in chosen souls to a higher level of excellence. They can hear the words of Christ: "Be ye perfect, as your heavenly Father is perfect",[10] and answer "I can do all in him who strengtheneth me",[11] for "Thou hast worked all our works in us".[12] Here too there are numberless degrees, but of the highest it may be truly said that when the hand of God through Christ is thus upon them they know and love with God's own

[9] I Cor. xv 41.
[10] Matt. v 48. Cf. Fourth Lateran Council (Denzinger ed. 28, n. 432): "Be ye perfect by perfection of grace as your heavenly Father is perfect by perfection of nature, each in his own manner."
[11] Philipp. iv 13.   [12] Isaiah xxvi 12.

knowledge and love. This knowledge, this love, is truly and strictly supernatural; it therefore exceeds all that can be expressed or felt by the faculties, but it is experienced by the soul, and when it has been thus experienced the recipient can endeavour to put into words what has happened.

Such, in barest outline, is the doctrine of Christian mysticism, but to make it a little more complete we may ask some questions which we shall find the English mystics pondering and answering. The first is, what is the relationship—if indeed any exists at all—between the normal self-discipline and practice of virtue which is certainly a part of all serious Christian life, and the contemplative life of which we have been speaking? We may put the question in other words and ask if all Christians should, or may, aspire to this life? Or are we to say, adapting the proverbial phrase, that a mystic is born and not made—born, that is, not of course by nature only, but by the hidden counsel of God, who allots to each his special task? A straight, unqualified answer, whether affirmative or negative, to either of these questions would seem to issue in a dilemma. That all Christians, or even all earnest Christians, should be called to such a life would seem to outrage the common sense of the religious, and not only of the worldly man. Moreover, it is the universal teaching of all the great masters that the mystical life is the pure gift of God, which cannot be deserved or expected by anyone, whatever his virtue. On the other hand, if we make the bare assertion that a mystic is in the spiritual sphere what a poet is in the human sphere, the possessor from birth of a faculty that cannot be desired and prayed for and hoped for during the labour and striving of a lifetime, we should be branding as useless and misleading not only the teaching of many of the greatest spiritual writers and contemplatives, but the teaching of Scripture itself.

In point of fact, these questions have not been, and probably cannot be, answered in any ready-made, smart fashion. They are closely bound up with the mystery which no human intelligence can probe, that of God's own choice of His elect and of the gifts given to each, for we are speaking of things that are not within the realm of unassisted human knowledge. On one point we may accept the unanimous evidence of mystics and theologians: that no one can hope, by his own effort assisted by God's grace, to attain in this life to mystical experience in the same way that he may hope and trust to attain to salvation. We may also accept the same testimony that mystical experience of the pure kind of which we have been speaking can only be attained by those who are themselves pure of heart: in other words, that the grace of contemplation is an extension, a "production" so to say, of the sanctifying grace of love, received together with faith at baptism and developed by the practice of the Christian virtues. May we go further, and say that there are, so to say, two families of mystics—those who, from childhood onwards, have been led by God's hand to the dark and silent waters of which St John of the Cross sang,[13] and those who have come to them at last by the long and hard way of evangelical service, the abandonment of all things and the choice of the Cross of Christ? Neither the theologians nor the mystics give us here a clear answer, but we may as historians and observers use the evidence we have acquired to suggest that this may be so.

A second question may have suggested itself to those readers who are familiar with the lives and writings of the saints. It is this: what connection, if any, has the mystical life as just described with the ecstasies, visions, locutions and extraordinary happenings of all kinds that fill so large a place in the current accounts of the lives of almost all the saints

[13] St John of the Cross, *Poems* viii (trans. Peers, 1 ed., II 454): "How well I know the fount that freely flows, Although 'tis night."

save those who have won their title by martyrdom? To most readers, even to most devout Christians, these are the signs and symptoms of the mystical life. Such happenings are, or seem to be, almost inseparably connected with the kind of sanctity officially honoured by the Church. Yet we are told, on the other hand, that such things form no part of the normal Christian life; that they are not essential to a holy life, and that the earnest Christian must not hope for, pray for or expect any such occurrences in his own life.

The same difficulty is found on a higher, theological level. If the pure mystical life has nothing to do with what can be heard, seen or felt by the human senses or faculties, what is to be said of the many theologians and other writers, including some of the saints accounted mystics, who seem to attach great importance to these things?

To answer these questions is probably the hardest of all the tasks of a mystical theologian, and even after so many centuries of Christian life it cannot be said that a clear and firm answer has yet been given. We are, after all, not dealing directly with a truth of revealed religion, but with the ways of God in dealing with individual human souls, and we can do no more than assemble the very imperfectly recorded experience of a relatively small number of men and women and, after having critically assessed its worth, endeavour to extract from it what seems to us to be the normal way in which the Holy Spirit leads souls. In what follows, we may be allowed to assume that God can communicate with and uplift His creatures in any way that pleases Him, and that we, for our part, can distinguish, at least in gross, between what is illusory and morbid, and what is authentic and sane.

We can therefore begin by noting the traditional distinction between what is called *gratia gratum faciens*—grace that makes the recipient well-pleasing to God, and is therefore an inward-working, sanctifying grace—and *gratia gratis data*—

grace that is given primarily for the benefit of others rather than of the recipient. The examples of this latter kind of grace are usually taken from the lists given by St Paul,[14] and include the gift of healing, the gifts of tongues, prophecy and miracles in general. These profit the recipient nothing, unless he has also divine charity,[15] but normally such gifts are in fact given to those who are pleasing to God, and in such a case they are accompanied by internal graces that guide and strengthen. We must also distinguish between a clear, external divine message and one directed to the individual soul. Scripture contains many examples of the first kind, such as the angelic messages to Zachary and to Our Lady; the message to Bernadette at Lourdes, if accepted as authentic, would seem to fall into this class, though it is not, of course, matter of divine revelation to be believed with divine faith, nor has it any of the authority that is possessed by Scripture. These messages in themselves are not mystical, though in the case of the Annunciation the external words of the archangel were doubtless accompanied by a superabundant internal enlightenment and enablement that would make the recipient able, in the familiar words of St Leo the Great, to conceive the Son of God in her mind before she conceived Him in her body.[16]

Our problem, therefore, is concerned with another type of religious experience, that of the intelligible message or clear though wordless impression communicated to the senses, imagination or intellect—what are called visions, locutions, raptures and the like. What is the nature and worth of these? Two answers have been given in the past. The one is, that as some of these impressions come from God these, when

[14] E.g. 1 Cor. xii.
[15] In such cases their use may be directed to the glory of God like any other good action.
[16] St Leo, *Sermo primus in Nativitate*. "Divinam humanamque prolem prius conciperet Maria mente quam corpore."

recognized, must be received gratefully; others are either purely natural or else the work of an evil spirit, and must therefore be rejected after expert examination. The other answer, given by many ancient and medieval spiritual guides and reasserted most emphatically by St John of the Cross, is more drastic. It is based on two principles, the one theological, the other philosophical. The first is, that God suits His gifts to the various degrees of advancement that souls have reached. The second, which in reality is another version of the first, is that whatever is received, depends for the manner of its reception upon the capacity and potentiality of the individual soul.[17] In other words, it is the imperfect human organism that receives perceptibly, but inadequately, the divine gift to the soul, and it receives it in such a way as to scale it down to its own capacity. On this view, the stronger and better prepared a soul may be, the less it perceives or adverts to what affects its natural faculties; the divine influence is there, and powerfully so, but it cannot be perceived by the mind in any expressible form. By the same token, an "ecstasy" is a weakness, a failure on the part of a soul that is not yet perfectly pure; the soul that is truly strong does not experience such things.

The first thought of many who come across this teaching is, that God's gifts, especially such high and unusual gifts, should not be neglected. We may, however, consider an analogous case on a lower level of spiritual life. The aesthetic, musical and literary beauties of the liturgy of the Church worthily performed in a noble setting are indeed reflections of God's beauty and are His gifts to win the mind and soul to a love of the Giver; but to allow the mind to rest in them when the soul might attain God more directly by faith and love would be to mistake the means for the end; it would be treachery to God Himself. St John's doctrine, which we shall

[17] "Quidquid recipitur, secundum modum recipientis recipitur."

find hinted also in our English mystics, shocks us only by reason of our lowliness and lack of living faith. He is looking to the heights, to the pure truth of God. We fail to see the invisible God behind His creatures, and are dazzled by what seems to be His direct presence, but is no more than another reflection in the distorting mirror of natural human weakness. Few, even of the saints, live always on the heights to which St John of the Cross directs our gaze, but on those heights are the two supreme models of our life, Our Lord and His Mother, who lived above all shadows, the one contemplating the very essence of God in His human soul, the other raised above all other creatures in grace and clarity of contemplation, yet each passing through the world entirely hidden, save to the eyes of faith.

But though this is so, such teaching can be appreciated as a practical, immediate norm of action only by those who are called and have the strength in one way or another to follow it. For them it is a necessary truth and duty, and unless they accept it they will not reach the depth of spiritual life attainable and the true mystical union. Others may be led by lower ways and many stages, and may go only a part of the way, in accordance with their call and their predestined grace. The ultimate criterion for all must be: that the will of God is alone to be considered, and that what does not tend to the union of the individual human will with the divine will is of no supernatural worth.

In the earlier part of this century there was a long and hard-fought controversy among theologians as to the "normality" of the vocation to the contemplative, "mystic", way. To one party the life of supernatural contemplation, the "mystical" life, was a normal, if in fact rare, prolongation of the common Christian life of sanctifying grace; all Christians were therefore called to it, at least remotely, by the very fact of their call to Christian perfection, and consequently they had fallen in some sense short of their vocation if, in a normal span of life, they had failed to reach their goal. This judgment would apply *a fortiori* to religious, who, by definition, are vowed to tend towards the perfection suitable to their state. To the other party the mystical life and the mystical graces were abnormal and special gifts to a few souls, and were without any intrinsic connection with sanctifying grace. Christian perfection, even of the heroic kind, could be attained without any specifically mystical graces, and perfection of this "non-mystical" kind, to which all Christians were at least remotely called, might be as high in degree, or even higher, than that of the mystics.

Behind this divergence of opinion lay a deep divergence in the theology of grace. To the former party sanctifying grace, from its beginning in baptism, was in essence fully and really supernatural, a new principle of life which could expand into the fully divinized life of the children of God. Though in the "common" life of Christians it did not supersede the normal human manner of thinking and acting, in perfect souls, given wholly to God, it replaced in growing measure the human manner of proceeding, so that the knowledge and love of the saints was truly "infused". In technical language, "co-operant" grace was superseded to a greater or less degree by "operant" grace. This was, in its essence, the direct action of God within the soul, moving it infallibly but freely in accordance with His good pleasure.

The second party, using a variety of expressions, regarded divine grace not as the divine action working infallibly within the human will, but as a divine assistance freely given and imparted in accordance with the divine foreknowledge of the individual's capabilities and actions. In the work of Christian perfection, therefore, the emphasis was set on the clarity of knowledge and the strength of the human will, which when assisted by grace would act and thereby merit yet further assistance. "Operant" grace was confined to the first justification of the soul; without the co-operation of the human will there could be no free, and therefore no meritorious, act. The mystical graces were consequently something beside and beyond normal co-operant grace; they were extra-normal "favours", incidents which had no intrinsic connection with the growth of the soul; technically speaking, they were to be classed with such graces as the gift of tongues or of prophecy. The first party, therefore, concentrated attention on the invisible, infallible (though not necessitating) interior working of grace as a purely supernatural principle of life, recognized in its effects but otherwise perceptible only to the eyes of faith; the other group emphasized the active co-operation of the human will, and confined the mystical life to the phenomena perceptible to the interior, if not to the exterior, senses and faculties.

As the years passed, the opponents drew gradually nearer to one another in position. The first party admitted more readily and completely the rarity of the true mystic, and the remoteness of the call to the contemplative life for all save a very small minority. On the other hand, by taking the deployment of the Gifts of the Holy Ghost as the theological criterion of mystical activity, they could find "mystical" modes of action in such "active" virtues as corresponded to the Gifts of counsel and fortitude, and thus the "supernatural mode" of the Gifts could be found in all holy souls. Since for them what distinguished the mystical life from the ordinary life of the virtuous sanctified soul was the action of the Holy Spirit, by means of the Gifts, moving the mind and will no longer imperceptibly, but perceptibly (at least in effect) with no precedent deliberation or effort, they were able to see in some saintly souls the working of the intellectual Gifts of Knowledge, Understanding and Wisdom, and in others that of the practical Gifts of Fear, Piety, Counsel and Fortitude. Their opponents, for their part, readily admitted an extension of the mystical field and at least a part of the action of the Gifts, thus making the "mystical element" a more important factor in the lives of the saints. The basic difference, however, remained, and resulted necessarily from the different ways of regarding sanctifying grace: the one party maintaining the essential continuity between the grace of baptism and the highest mystical graces, while the other still considered mystical graces as isolated favours standing outside, or at best parallel to, the normal life of sanctifying grace which, even when prolonged to heroic sanctity, was regarded as a series of aids and dispositions rather than as a vital principle. There was still a tendency among those who thought thus to postulate two "ways" to sanctity, the mystical and the non-mystical, and to maintain that there was an equality between them.

To one standing outside the theological controversy it may well seem that the first of the two parties is fully justified both from theological principles and from the writings of the mystics, in regarding the growth of grace as a continuous progress, and in asserting that the soul only reaches the fullness of perfection when its task consists primarily in receiving, knowingly and willingly, the action of God upon and within it, first as a purifying force and later as a moving and illuminating agent. It is, however, not necessary to deduce from this that all Christian souls or even all those vowed to the religious life are called in any real or immediate sense to the mystical life. The argument drawn from tradition in this matter is not convincing, as will perhaps be seen in the following chapter. The early Christian mystical writings were "contaminated" from Neoplatonic sources, in which there was no conception of the infinite distance between God and man, and in which contemplation was a higher activity, indeed, but one not wholly outside the range of the soul's capacity. Moreover, though the theologians in question are justified in regarding the mystical graces of the Gifts as a superior kind of sanctifying grace, and justified in consequence in their unwillingness to admit two kinds of perfection, the ascetic and the mystical, they do not always emphasize sufficiently the variety of gifts and vocations in the Church, and do not state clearly enough that the God-given capacity to receive is as important a determining factor as the God-given grace that is received. Also, perhaps, they fail to take sufficient notice of the part played by the passive purification of the soul by the divine action upon it in the form of the light of unitive contemplation which is at first felt as an overwhelming, constrictive, punitive force. Of this there is no trace in the over-intellectualized system of the Neo-platonists, in which the negation of all that is not-God is followed inevitably by the inflowing of the divine. When all has been said, there is something in us that recoils from at least the more extreme forms of the teaching of the universal invitation to the mystical life. While it is certainly the antecedent will of God that all men should be saved, and only the consequent will of God that those who culpably fail God under certain conditions should be lost, it can scarcely be thought to be the antecedent will of God that all should attain in this life to contemplation. While it is indeed true that many are called, and few chosen, it is also true that star differs from star in glory, and that to one are given more talents than another may receive.

To a theologian, the mystical life is distinguished from the life of any Christian in a state of grace by the soul's manner of responding to God's action. The Christian in the common state of grace co-operates with the grace of God in thinking and acting in a normal human manner, but with his actions directed by his will under the influence of the theological virtues to a supernatural end and object, the love and service of God as He is made known by revelation. Such a one believes in and loves the invisible God, but he has no immediate, direct awareness of God's action upon or in him. When, however, partly by its own efforts, assisted by grace, and partly by the direct action of God upon it, a soul has freed itself from all inordinate love of, and advertence to, anything apart from God, the divine agency, the Holy Spirit, may take possession of its faculties and "infuse" love and knowledge to which the recipient opposes no barrier; he has strength to bear this infusion, this contact with God, and the purity to accept it. He becomes to a greater or less extent united in will and love with God. As one so united he is, far more truly than before, a fully developed personality, since he not only realizes to the full his natural potentialities, but also liberates for God's action upon it the *potentia obedientialis*, the capacity of the creature to receive powers of a supernatural kind in obedience and submission to God.

On the empirical level, the mystical life is usually distinguished by an awareness, on the part of the individual concerned, of the existence of the soul at a deeper level than that of ordinary mental consciousness, and often also of the indwelling of God, the Three Divine Persons, within it. The mystic is also aware of spiritual beings of all kinds—of the souls of others seen as something other than their minds or perceptible human characteristics, and of the spiritual world of good and evil.[18] As regards prayer, which is normally, though perhaps not altogether desirably, taken by writers on mystical theology as the ruling index of spiritual development, the progress from "ordinary" to "mystical" prayer, which follows concurrently with a growth in the virtues of faith, hope and charity, and the appearance of the "super-

[18] St John of the Cross, *Spiritual Canticle* (second redaction) stanza xvi par. 6 (trans. Peers II 278): "When the soul becomes very greatly detached in spirit . . . the devil can readily appear to it, since he is likewise a spirit." *Dark Night* II xxiii par. 5 (Peers I 478): "When there is a naked contact of spirit with spirit, the horror is intolerable which the evil spirit causes in the soul."

natural mode of action" of the Gifts of the Holy Spirit, consists of a growing simplicity and power of recollection, and
passes first from the "ordinary" prayer of discrete movements
of the mind and will to the prayer, not yet mystical and yet
not habitually within the capacity of all Christians, of a
simple, continuous, loving attendance upon God. The truly
mystical initial prayer is distinguished from this by an awareness of a love and knowledge and "presence" of God that
does not proceed from any thought or conscious motive, but
is in the soul without the previous activity of its faculties.
Beyond this, the development of the mystical life can be
followed in the classical account of St John of the Cross and
the theologians who follow him.

The mystical life must always remain indescribable and incomprehensible to those who stand without. We are confronted by a double danger, that of ignoring or distrusting
what we do not understand, and that of exalting the smallest
appearance of what is unfamiliar—*omne ignotum pro magnifico*.
We may err by regarding as marvellous what is in fact of
little or no significance, or we may on the other hand regard
as ordinary or negligible what is in fact most precious and
most holy. Or we may in a kind of desperation regard all of
which we have no experience as equally insignificant. If we
would do the barest justice to the importance of the matter
we must be prepared to use the most searching criticism and
at the same time to recognize the true sublime. While we
must not be deceived by words, or by every account of
signs and wonders, we must recognize real worth wherever
it is found.

Perhaps at the present time there is a tendency among
spiritual writers to lower unduly the threshold of contemplation, to encourage souls to think that one who practises the
prayer of simplicity or of loving attention—or even any
formless kind of affective prayer—may take to himself the

name and prerogatives of a contemplative. Such a degrada-
tion sooner or later produces a disregard, even a distrust, of
the true mystical life, and there is always the danger of
"quietism", not indeed in the gross and extravagant forms
condemned in the seventeenth century, but in the form of
applying the teaching of the saints—and the English mystics—
to low and commonplace levels of the spiritual life. And
though the growth in grace, like all spiritual growth of
which we have experience, is normally a slow and continuous
process, yet there is a moment, as there is in the process of
conversion from sin or unbelief, when the soul realizes and
marvels that the right hand of the Lord hath wrought power,
and that a new chapter of life is opening. This real birth of
the mystical life, rare but real, must not be confused or
blurred by identification with a mere facility for prayer or an
inability to make set meditations.

Above all, we must not blaspheme what we do not understand:

> Since rare occurrences, of which few have had experience,
> seem for these very reasons the more marvellous and the less
> credible . . . I do not doubt that certain persons, who under-
> stand it not through their learning, neither know it by ex-
> perience, will either disbelieve it or will consider it to be
> exaggerated, or will think that it is not in itself as great a thing
> as it is.[19]

[19] St John of the Cross, *Living Flame*, stanza, I § 15, 2 redaction (Peers III 125).

Chapter II

THE EVOLUTION OF CATHOLIC MYSTICAL THEOLOGY

THE essence of Christian mysticism, the real but super-natural union between the soul, with its powers of knowledge and love, and God, has been one and the same since the Incarnation. To analyse and to describe it must always be difficult, for the experience itself is rare and by definition supernatural and ineffable, but such attempts need not lead to confusion if the words of the mystics themselves are faithfully and critically examined and the principles of traditional theology understood and followed. To write an historical account, however, not precisely of Christian mysticism but of the evolution of Christian mystical theology is a very different matter, for in this case the pure stream of un-sophisticated Christian experience has been contaminated again and again from sources extraneous to Christianity. Contemplation, in particular, the central term and concept of mystical theology, has been from the very beginning a treacherous and equivocal word.

Greek philosophy, and in particular the thought of Plato and Aristotle which had the greatest and most permanent vogue among early Christian thinkers, was the philosophy of a race distinguished above all others by its intellectual power, and of men to whom the universe of thought and spirit was more real than that of sense and matter, and to whom the speculative intellect was the highest power of man. In consequence, man's highest activity and the goal of his endeavour was a life, either here or hereafter, spent in the intellectual vision of truth, or, to use the phrase employed by Aristotle, in the life of contemplation. In Plato's dialogues, and throughout the works of Aristotle, this was a natural, intellectual, human activity, and as such available to all with the necessary mental power and moral preparation, but in later Platonism and in particular in the scheme of Plotinus and the Neoplatonists, this life of contemplation acquired a more distinctly religious character, partly through a particular interpretation of some of the Platonic dialogues, partly through the construction of a metaphysical system which had at its summit the One who was also called God, and partly through the specifically religious and mystical interests of Plotinus himself. For Plotinus the universe of spirit, and in particular the individual human soul, yearned to return to Mind from which it had come forth and to contemplate, in union with Mind, Mind itself, the author and exemplar of being, truth and goodness. This contemplation, in the life beyond this life, would be a purely intellectual contemplation of the object that fully satisfied the powers of the soul, and thus, strictly speaking, connatural to the soul, but Plotinus himself described yet a further degree of spiritual life in which the soul went out of itself, or rather was drawn out of itself, in ecstasy to the One above all being, and thus attained to a union wholly ineffable which was one of love as well as, perhaps rather than, one of intellection. Here we see clearly for the first time three assertions or principles, propounded by a non-Christian philosopher, that were to influence so deeply the expression of Christian mystical theology: the contemplative life as the goal above all other activities for the human soul; the intellectual contemplation of divine truth; and the God-given, ecstatic, ineffable union of love.

Meanwhile, even before the lifetime of Plotinus, the school of Christian Platonists at Alexandria, themselves drawing upon the Jewish Platonist Philo and the writings of the later Academy, were applying Platonic principles to the Christian life. Origen, and his follower Clement of Alexandria, made a clear distinction between the active life of faith, good works and virtues, leading to a perfect peace and liberty of spirit through renunciation and mortification of the desires, and the resultant superior state of the perfect love of God and the contemplative life. They thus taught that above the bare adherence to the doctrines of the faith as presented to all fully initiated Christians, there was a spiritual understanding of these doctrines and of Holy Scripture, the result of an illumination by a fuller grace in pure souls, which surpassed that of bare faith. This they called *gnosis* (knowledge) and later the term *theoria* (contemplation) was used, and its exercise was regarded as the worthiest employment of a Christian soul, though few were qualified to enjoy it. While it is clear that in the minds of those who propounded it, this contemplation was the outcome of a special grace, and therefore fully Christian and supernatural, it is not certain that, as presented by the Alexandrians, it was strictly mystical: that is, a wholly God-given experience of the union of the mind and will with God. To later ages it seems rather to have been considered as a divinely assisted penetration of the mysteries and a consequent speculation upon them.

When, however, the Alexandrian teaching spread in the Asian church, it was developed by the great Cappadocian doctors and particularly by St Gregory of Nyssa, in whose writings the fully supernatural experience of union with God is clearly enunciated, and who has in consequence been called "the father of Christian mysticism". He distinguishes clearly between the active life and prayer of the workaday Christian, the still active prayer in which the mind encounters a cloud or darkness above itself, and the gratuitous, wholly supernatural attainment of God present by faith as a presence experienced in darkness; above this still is ecstasy, the mind going out of itself to the unknowable.

This teaching was to have a great future. Among those who first made use of it was a disciple of St Basil and St Gregory Nazianzen, Evagrius of Pontus (356–399), who became a monk of Egypt and a disciple of St Macarius, and who gave to the monastic East a doctrine of the contemplative life in which we may recognize elements from the Alexandrians as well as from Gregory of Nyssa. In the scheme of ascesis and prayer elaborated by him, the active, practical pursuit of virtue is followed by a meditation upon the works of God (*theoria*) and that in turn by the "theology" or contemplation of rational creatures and of God. This last is not within man's unaided power, but is God-given. Evagrius is insistent that nothing perceptible by man or accessible to man by his human powers is God.

Alongside of this teaching, the fathers of the desert were providing for their disciples instruction on common and on contemplative or mystical prayer based solely or chiefly on personal experience with no admixture of extraneous theory. Here for the first time there appear almost all the elements that occur in later spiritual systems of ascesis and prayer in different measure: the active pursuit of the virtues accompanied by abnegation of all kinds; the progress towards recollection and the transcendence of things pleasurable and painful; the gradual attainment of purity of heart; an insistence on the intimate connection between the growth in virtues, particularly those of charity and faith, and the advance in purity and facility in prayer; and, finally, the all-important recognition of a direct, experienced divine assistance making possible a kind of prayer and a mode of virtuous living and acting of which human nature, even when trained and purified and assisted by "ordinary" grace, must remain incapable. There are, in the documents giving the teaching of these fathers, several clear descriptions of infused contemplative prayer and of the infused recollection of the powers of the soul. The emphasis throughout is laid on the Christian life and the Christian mysteries, and on the gradual progress of the soul towards God, seen either as the Father or the Incarnate Son, and though there are traces of the Alexandrian degrees of contemplation and of the need for "apathy", or indifference, these remain little more than traces, and ecstasy, when mentioned, is closer to the ecstasy of more recent mystical writers than to that of Neoplatonism. Cassian, in his reportage of the experiences of the fathers of the desert, remains almost always sober and practical, and it is not to be wondered at that he should have remained throughout the middle ages and down to modern times a principal guide for fervent souls. Had Cassian and the other writings of the desert remained the only literary inheritance of the ancient world to exercise its influence over posterity, mystical theology and its terminology might have remained a simpler and a more comprehensible discipline than it has in fact proved to be. The practical tradition, in the event, was confused by two very influential writers, St Augustine and Dionysius the pseudo-Areopagite.

St Augustine had no occasion to give elaborate instructions on prayer and on the degrees of the spiritual life. On the other hand, he described in detail some of his own spiritual experiences; he also laid down the programme of a Christian education which in its higher reaches merged into a psychological and spiritual ascent towards God; and he discussed at length the relationship of the active and contemplative lives. On all these topics what he wrote inevitably came to have great weight with subsequent writers, and, indeed, gave its characteristic bent to a long medieval tradition.

Augustine's theological descriptions of the manner of the soul's attainment to the direct knowledge of God, and his accounts of his personal experiences are, as all acknowledge, documents of the greatest power and interest, but as soon as attention had been drawn towards them, by Abbot Cuthbert Butler and others, as crucial evidence for the mystical life of their author, a wide difference of opinion made itself felt as to their precise significance. This division affected Catholic theologians as much as others and, to judge from a recent authoritative survey, any kind of general agreement is still out of sight. On the one hand the resemblances, often so close as to be verbal, to passages in Plotinus and Porphyry would seem to imply that the experiences described are identical, and this would give pause to some (though not to all) of those who are looking in Augustine's words for a fully super-natural mystical experience. We may add also that some of these experiences occurred either before or shortly after Augustine's conversion and baptism, when we should scarcely expect to meet with advanced mystical experiences, while other descriptions of his feelings at the time were certainly written many years after the occurrence of the events they describe. On the other hand, almost all these passages contain phrases which if used by a writer of today, or of the last two centuries, would certainly denote a religious experience outside the purview of even devout and sincere souls who are not themselves mystics. Abbot Cuthbert Butler, who faced the question very resolutely almost thirty years ago, came down quite firmly in favour of a fully mystical experience, but his reiteration that the question is "not really in doubt" or is "beyond all possibility of doubt", and that such and such a passage "unquestionably describes the mystical experience", has not had the effect of silencing all gainsayers. Neither the problem itself, nor even the state of the question, can be resolved here, but it may be remarked, firstly, that an intense, though not technically speaking a mystical experience, retailed by such a delicately perceptive mind with such an unparalleled mastery of language as was Augustine's, might well take on a fire and a life that would lead the reader to rate it more highly than a careful theologian might allow, and secondly, that it is possible that Augustine is on occasion describing a supernatural, but not a strictly mystical, enlightenment such as St John of the Cross and others have described. This might take one of two forms: either what may be called the general supernatural enlightenment of every Christian mind in proportion to its purity and degree of charity; or the occasional intellectual enlightenment regarding God Himself and other truths given to the mind in an experiential, but not a strictly mystical, way.

This latter interpretation of St Augustine's description of his own experience may find some support from his scheme of Christian education. This, though it begins with elements of grammatical and mental training such as might be found in any educational programme, soon develops into a guide for the Christian mind in its ascent to God. Once again, the Plotinian influence is obvious and the theological implications doubtful. Augustine recognized with Plotinus three ordinary and one extraordinary degree of knowledge: the knowledge of creatures by science; the knowledge of Scripture and theology by wisdom; and the knowledge of the supreme, immutable Truth by intuition. Finally, above these is the mystical, ineffable union of the mind with God. But throughout, even when he seems to be proceeding most formally, Augustine is in fact describing the psychological findings of his own life, and he has in mind the individual soul in act, with all the intermingling and blending of grace and nature that is present in the living spirit. Seven hundred years later, however, when his works were being read as the authoritative text-books on every subject that they touched, his scheme, with its wholly spiritual, extra-temporal, aim, was taken as the model for a Christian life of study, and the Victorines, and St Bonaventure, together with many others, adapted it to their own purposes. In this scheme of Augustine, both the second and the third degrees of knowledge were parts of the "contemplative" life, and this helped greatly to widen, and in time to confuse, the meaning of the term.

Finally, the influence of St Augustine made itself felt, firmly and permanently, in the discussion of the relations between the contemplative and active lives. Augustine's fullest exposition, which became a *locus classicus*, is to be found in a series of sermons in his long commentary on the gospel of St John. The topic was started by the words of Christ to Peter and John recorded in the last chapter, and Augustine expatiated also on the contrasted occupations of the sisters of Lazarus, who had long been types of the active and contemplative lives. Throughout his writings Augustine compared the pursuits and worth of the "two lives divinely preached and commended" to the Church, and in so doing he became the fount and origin of the vexatious ambiguity of terminology that has persisted to the present day. For Augustine in this context the contemplative life is a life of study, meditation and reflection; it is the Platonic and Aristotelian life of contemplation translated into Christian terms. It is not the life of a mystic as such, but the life of one given to the consideration of Scripture and theology as understood in Augustine's scheme of the Christian's intellectual ascent to God; its goal is indeed the vision of God, dimly here and clearly hereafter, but it is a way of life in its external totality, the life of a whole class of Christians, not the mystical progress of divinely called individuals. While it might foster a life of mystical prayer, this would not be its direct or inevitable end. Indeed, the active and contemplative lives of Augustine have the same kind of relationship to categories of the individual's spiritual life as his two Cities have to the Church and State—they are on a different level of existence. In the sequel, the Augustinian division of the two lives, stereotyped by a long succession of derivative authorities, became standard in the designation of pursuits and in the classification of religious orders, with the consequent ambiguity that has permeated every branch of religious literature and confused numberless controversies and classifications.

This threefold influence of Augustine was not felt immediately, but it won its way gradually as the great doctor became the paramount authority in every department of theology and religious writing. Meanwhile another body of writing, destined to have a great future, had come into existence in the eastern church under the name of Dionysius the Areopagite.

This anonymous personage, probably a Syrian monk writing c. A.D. 500, based his teaching, as has recently been proved to demonstration, principally upon the works of St Gregory of Nyssa and, through him, on the Alexandrian Platonists, but he also made use of Neoplatonism as it existed in the final form given to it by Proclus. Though himself an orthodox Christian, Dionysius adopted many of the Neoplatonic conceptions. Thus for him God is above all that can be attributed to him of perfections, and is even above being itself. He is the One, ineffable, inexpressible, unknowable, and Dionysius expounds on the one hand the Plotinian circle of the outgoing of all being from God, followed by its return, and the later Neoplatonist conception of the hierarchy of spirits, human and angelic, in which each order receives illumination from the rank above, and passes it down in diluted form to its inferior. This teaching, in so far as it concerned angelic beings, was to be integrated by St Thomas into the Christian framework, but its chief influence was upon speculative theologians. On the topic of mystical theology Dionysius's short treatise of that name was destined to have an immense influence, for it exactly filled, or seemed to fill, a gap in the teaching of the Western Fathers.

In his *Mystical Theology* Dionysius uses the hierarchy of being as stages in the ladder of denial to be climbed by the soul in its ascent to God. Christianizing the spiritual ascent of Plotinus, he leads the soul from the beauties of creation to the hierarchy of spiritual beings and thence to a God-given contemplation of the divine names and the "things of God", that is, in effect, the divinity as "broken down" by our inadequate powers of cognition. In all this we can recognize a parallelism with Augustine, though the idiom of the two writers is not the same. But whereas for Augustine God is clearly and explicitly the God of the Old and New Testaments, Father of all and the Light that enlightens every man, with Dionysius he is still the super-essential, ineffable One, and whereas for Augustine the Christian may attain to a momentary glimpse of uncreated light, with Dionysius he may, but only rarely and briefly, experience the ecstatic Plotinian going forth to the divine darkness, and to union in that darkness with God. Two phrases of Dionysius, characteristic in themselves, became firmly embedded in Western tradition, the "ray of darkness" and the "cloud of unknowing". Whether in fact the Dionysian ecstasy is the same as the Christian mystical union, whether Dionysius himself was a mystic, or merely a mystical theologian, and whether the Dionysian scheme can be equated in any real sense with the Augustinian, are questions that have not as yet been finally answered; they share the ambiguity that affects all systems built upon the Plotinian model.

For six hundred years after the lifetime of Dionysius mystical theology, whether speculative or descriptive, remained stagnant in the west along with all other kinds of intellectual activity. No doubt a succession of souls, some well known to their contemporaries while others were hidden, were called to the mystical life; they had for their guide the Scriptures and the old monastic traditions and, above all, the sacraments of the Church and the light of the Holy Spirit. But on the formal, explicit, literary level anything that was written repeated in weakened solution the teaching of St Augustine, and his stages of the Christian's enlightenment gradually became degrees of the monastic ascesis, and his stages of science, wisdom and intuition were replaced by the reading, meditation and contemplation which generations of writers rehearsed without discussing or defining the meaning of what they wrote.

With the intellectual and spiritual revival of the eleventh and twelfth centuries a great change came which manifested itself in three principal ways. The traditional, largely Augustinian, doctrine was subjected to treatment at the hands of those trained in the new dialectic, with its predilection for analysis and formalization; the works of Dionysius, and in particular the *Mystical Theology*, were influential with the Victorines and the Cistercians; and the conventions of the new age permitted once more the narration of personal experience freed from traditional formalization. Of this last kind of writing the most celebrated example was St Bernard's description of his own mystical experiences in his *Sermons on the Canticle*, which anticipates so much of the self-revelation of later centuries. The theory of the mystical life was elaborated by many writers, and above all by the two great Victorines, Hugh and Richard, and in an epoch of authoritative text-books Richard's *Benjamin Major* and still more his *Benjamin Minor* became and remained classics in every library. They were in essence traditionally Augustinian, though the emphasis was shifted from the mental and intellectual life of the Christian to the specifically devotional and spiritual, and the influence of Dionysius became apparent. The contemplative life was represented as a progress from meditation through a long process of abstraction to contemplation, and thence to the supreme ecstasy. Richard of

St Victor, however, in blending the Augustinian and Dionysian traditions, made two significant, though perhaps not
fully intentional, modifications. The "cloud of darkness",
which in Dionysius was the super-essential God, becomes in
Richard a twofold cloud of much less metaphysical import:
on the one hand the cloud of forgetfulness of creatures beneath the soul, and on the other the cloud of unknowing in
God which could be pierced to emit rays of light; and
yet the almost exclusively intellectual process of Dionysius
becomes under Augustinian influence strongly affective,
the work of the will, a work of love. Nevertheless with
Richard, as with all those in the past who drew upon
Neoplatonism, the supreme ecstasy is rare and short.

For another hundred years the Augustinian tradition continued to develop, reaching its clearest and most magisterial
shape in St Bonaventure's *Itinerarium Mentis ad Deum*. This,
and indeed the whole programme of St Bonaventure, was a
powerful and genial re-statement in terms of the thirteenth
century scholastic world, of St Augustine's programme of
Christian knowledge and wisdom, greatly reinforced and
made more actual by the infusion of direct Franciscan experience, the simple, direct, loving imitation of the crucified
Jesus. Regarded from the purely speculative angle, it had
many of the characteristics present in St Augustine's thought,
and in particular the great doctor's conception of the Christian's soul-life (a projection of his own soul and life) as a
single, richly endowed, grace-enlightened, unified and
dynamic activity. Such a conception, psychologically and
existentially attractive to a degree, is something quite different from that of the analytic theologian who is engaged upon
defining the degrees of the spiritual life, or from that of the
spiritual director concerned with the specific instructions to
be given to those at different stages of the soul's growth.
These two latter classes were, however, becoming more and

more important, the former among the Aristotelian theologians, the latter among the classes to whom the traditional monastic ascesis of a life lived in a strict routine of obedience was no longer fully applicable to a world of ever-growing complexity and to a devout class outside the walls of a monastery of the ancient orders.

If Richard of St Victor gave scholastic shape to the traditional Augustinian scheme of the contemplative life, he was also one of the first among the scholastics to be influenced by the teaching of Dionysius. If he takes the doctrine of the active and contemplative lives, and of the various types of vision, from Augustine, the use he makes of the entry of Moses into the cloud where God dwelt, whom it was not lawful to see, and the emphasis on the ecstasy in which man loses himself in God, came from Dionysius. Meanwhile, the translations of Dionysius were multiplied, and among them was that of Sarracenus accompanied by a commentary of Thomas Gallus, in origin a canon from St Victor's at Paris. He completed the process begun by Richard, and laid all the emphasis upon the will and upon love in the beginning of the life of contemplation and in the final attainment of union with God. As a result, the masters of the early fourteenth century who inherited both the Victorine (and Augustinian) tradition and the newly found Dionysian corpus, were never confronted with the difficulty of harmonizing the intellectualist bias of the Greek with the affective tendency of Augustine and the school of Bonaventure, for the task had been largely accomplished for them by the editors of Dionysius.

All the writers of whom we have just been speaking were in greater or less degree theoreticians. The Victorines in particular, and their followers, though perhaps themselves men of deep spiritual life, presented the life of contemplation in a schematized, formal fashion that could have been of little help to a soul who wished to live the life of contemplation, not to pass an examination upon it or himself to write upon it. The need for something more simple and more practical grew as the decades passed, and became more and more insistent as the populations of the northern towns and cities increased and the number of the devout grew. It was in these circumstances that a new and epoch-making school of mystical theologians and spiritual directors arose among the Dominican friars of the Rhineland. In the cities of south Germany there were numerous convents of women not under the Rule or direction of one of the older orders; there were also numerous quasi-heretical or extravagant religious sects and groups there; and in consequence Pope Clement IV in 1267 gave command that learned members of the Dominican order should act as spiritual directors of the nuns. The obligation was twice repeated by the provincial of Germany before the end of the century. It was in all probability owing to this direct command that the great Dominican school of spiritual teaching owed its rise; it was destined to produce in rapid succession three of the greatest mystical writers of the Middle Ages, and to influence profoundly all subsequent Catholic spirituality.

The Rhineland Dominicans had at this time a philosophical and theological outlook which differed considerably from that of other provinces. Albert the Great, during his residence as regent at Cologne, had absorbed large doses of Neoplatonic teaching from the early thirteenth-century translators and also from the new translations of William of Moerbeke. The works so translated included a treatise of Proclus (of which Albert was probably unaware), the whole of the Dionysian corpus, and scattered pieces of Plotinus and Porphyry. Albert's disciples, and in particular Dietrich of Freiberg, continued the tradition and elaborated an epistemology and a theory of the "basic" soul, the image of God, the "spark",

which was to be a specific mark of the school. Master Eckhardt carried the Neoplatonist theology still further in a
system of great complexity and difficulty, in which a wholly
Neoplatonist metaphysic and mystical speculation was worked
by a machinery of Thomist axioms and arguments. Scholars
and theologians are still divided in their judgments both as to
the nature of the doctrines and the orthodoxy of Eckhardt,
and there is also division of opinion as to whether he was
himself a distinguished mystic or merely a theologian who
wrapped his deeply religious speculations in Dionysian garb.
Here we are concerned only to note that alongside of his
theological teaching he was a tireless and influential preacher
and spiritual guide. It was not, however, Eckhardt who left
a permanent mark upon the practice of Catholic spirituality,
but his disciple John Tauler. Tauler, while never losing his
admiration for Eckhardt, did in fact take less interest in the
speculative side of his teaching, and himself adopted more
fully the Thomist doctrine of the clear distinction between
the realm of nature and that of grace. He was primarily, in
such works as have come down to us, concerned with moral
and spiritual reformation, and must take rank as one of the
greatest preachers and spiritual directors of the middle ages.
Penetrated as he was by Dionysian doctrines, he gave to all
his hearers, whether enclosed religious or devout layfolk, the
invitation to, and instructions for, the contemplative life,
which he regarded, following the Neoplatonist tradition, as
the normal consummation of the Christian life of perfection
and as an inflowing of the divine light that took place, in
God's freely ordained disposition of things, as soon as the
receptacle of the soul had been prepared by the removal of
all obstacles to God's grace. He also received from Dionysius
the doctrine of the cloud of unknowing, which became for
him something very like the night of the soul in the writings
of St John of the Cross. Tauler, as a theologian, was in most

matters an orthodox Thomist, and held therefore the Thomist doctrine of the capacity of the soul to attain directly to God by the theological virtue of charity, and his practical teaching is full of insistence on the value of a prayer that is "naked" love or "naked" intent directed to a God hidden in the darkness of faith.

Finally, a word may be said of the influence of St Thomas himself on mystical theology. St Thomas in many respects stands half-way between the theoretical Augustinians of the school of the Victorines and the practical, personal outlook of the German group. Though he nowhere deals at length with the stages of the spiritual life, he has many articles on contemplation, and these have been the centre of much discussion in recent times. Broadly speaking, contemplation is for him the contemplation of St Augustine and Dionysius, that is, the supernaturally enlightened penetration of the Scriptures and Christian doctrine by the mind purified by the practice of the virtues, particularly those of faith and charity. This, considered without reference to other passages in his writings, might be thought to have little connection with the mysticism of Tauler, but St Thomas is of importance in the history of Christian spirituality by reason of other aspects of his teaching. In his exposition of the working of grace he distinguishes between the grace that is the normal co-operative element in the virtuous act of a Christian and the higher form of grace, the so-called "operant" grace, which supersedes the natural, active powers in a sanctified soul and accomplishes its function within the freely consenting soul. St Thomas went a stage further, and attributed this kind of divine action to the free and full functioning of the Gifts of the Holy Spirit, which in their manner of acting surpassed even the theological virtues of faith, hope and charity. Among them the Gifts of Understanding and Wisdom were the noblest, and primarily concerned with the knowing powers of the soul, though the highest form of knowledge came also through love.

St Thomas had no occasion to apply his teaching on the Gifts systematically to a scheme of mystical theology, but the Thomist school, and in particular the Germans, applied his teaching on the two kinds of grace to the active and contemplative lives respectively, with far-reaching implications that were, as we shall see, realized in part by some of the English mystics, and were fully developed in the sixteenth century. As for the Thomist doctrine of the Gifts, this remained unexploited by the theologians who were deeply influenced by the Neoplatonists and Dionysius, but was to have its day in the mystical *Summae* of the Counter-Reformation.

We may perhaps sum up this rapid survey by noting that at the beginning of the fourteenth century two streams of doctrine were at least potentially available for trained minds. There was the Augustinian scheme, formalized by the Victorines, in which contemplation was a half intellectual, half devotional, grace-enlightened penetration of Christian truth, the normal, if somewhat uncommon, result of long ascetic and mental preparation. Beyond this was the fully mystical, transient, ecstatic experience. There was also the scheme of the German Dominican masters, based chiefly on Christianized Neoplatonist teaching, in which contemplation, the fully mystical contemplation of God in darkness, was accompanied by a new, infused love and knowledge, real but incommunicable. Beneath both these schools of doctrine there lay in the concrete, individual case the age-old, traditional, practical instruction on the ascetic life and the life of prayer that had become explicit among the Fathers of the desert and had remained current throughout the ages. We shall see in the English mystics, in varying degrees and measures, these three strands, themselves woven of many threads, uniting to compose the pattern of the spiritual life that appears when we read their writings. In Rolle we have the personal, un-theological account of personal experience, never fully in-tegrated into the traditional scheme of St Augustine and the Victorines which he takes as his doctrinal basis. In *The Cloud* and its companions we have the first great English spiritual director, deeply influenced by the Dominican school of Thomist theology and by the mystical teaching of Tauler, yet with a stream of traditional ornament derived from the Victorines and St Augustine. In Hilton we see a development of the Rhineland tradition set in a framework of the monastic and contemplative teaching of the earlier centuries. In Julian we have the direct personal experience, stimulated perhaps by the writings of the women visionaries of Germany and the Netherlands, and controlled by the eclectic, well-informed spiritual directors of East Anglia.

Chapter III

THE ENGLAND OF THE MYSTICS

IN order to appreciate the significance of the English medieval mystics it is necessary to know something of the social and religious background of their age, and of the state of the Church in England both in their day and in earlier times.

To the student of history who reads only the text-books or the paper-backs of English academic historians, the fourteenth century may seem a period lacking in great designs and achievements, and far less attractive as a subject for close study than, say, the thirteenth or the sixteenth. It is not a century of great beginnings or mature achievements. The political and constitutional events are often confused and disjointed. Owing partly to plagues and partly to causes that lie too deep for observation, it was a time of economic and demographic recession and, to some extent, of frustration, for the years of agricultural and pastoral expansion were giving way to a time when labour was becoming scarce and the wool-trade was thrown out of balance by war and by the financial demands which war brought about.

At the same time, the last quarter of the century was marked by movements of discontent more widely spread and more influential than the debates on national policy and the passing feuds and intrigues around the king. There was the rising of the peasants in 1381, the first disturbance of its kind in England, which shook the whole fabric of society for a moment, though it was not in fact to be the prelude of a revolution. There was also a general discontent among the official and merchant classes, brought about by the long and latterly unsuccessful warfare, and expressing itself in an attack on the possessions and financial claims of the Pope, the bishops and the religious orders. This again, though a presage of things to come, did not in fact lead to any immediate spoliation or schism. Finally, there was the emergence of a full-scale attack upon important sectors of traditional Catholic theology and hierocracy by Wyclif, and the subsequent appearance of a radical and missionary religious movement appealing particularly to layfolk which, if successful, would have been revolutionary in its effects. This also was in the sequel contained by the firm action of authority, but was extremely significant, not only as giving a clear programme of anti-papal and in some respects anti-Catholic policy, but as marking the first appearance of a type of religious thought and sentiment, earnest and zealous, anti-sacramental and anti-sacerdotal, that was later to become and to remain characteristic of a large part of the population of England under the various banners of Puritanism, Independence, Dissent, Nonconformity and Free Churchmanship.

To contemporaries, indeed, and to historians of the past, the age of the famous victories in France, and of the displays of chivalry at home, was one of national glory and pride, and certainly it was in the fourteenth century that England for the first time became conscious of its nationhood, but more recent writers have emphasized the aftermath of the war—financial stringency, political and personal intrigues, commercial changes and the deterioration of ideals that a long war always brings. The epoch that opened with the unworthiness of Edward II and closed with the extravagance of Richard II is not, for most students, one of significant endeavour or notable achievement.

This, however, is not the whole picture of the age. In architecture and the allied arts, in speculative thought, and in vernacular literature the century was in every way productive of works equal or superior to anything that had gone before. Its first half saw the perfection of the mature "decorated" style in Gothic architecture with the lantern and Lady Chapel at Ely, the central tower and Lady Chapel at Wells, and the spires of Salisbury, Norwich, Chichester and Lichfield; in its second half the most original and characteristic of English styles, the so-called "perpendicular", appeared in London, Westminster and Gloucester, and achieved recognition in the naves of Canterbury and Winchester cathedrals. In philosophical and theological fields England gave to Europe in Duns Scotus, who was still young in 1300, and William of Ockham the two thinkers who were between them to divide the allegiance of the schools for two hundred years. In mathematics and kindred sciences the series of great Mertonians at Oxford, Thomas Bradwardine, Richard Swineshead, William Heytesbury and Ralph Strood were the masters of the academic world of their day. In poetry it was the first great age of English literature, in which not only Langland and Chaucer, but several other anonymous writers, touched absolute greatness and a height of poetic genius not reached again till the days of Spenser and Marlowe two hundred years later.

Yet despite these striking and positive achievements, the age was not in all respects one of growth and advance. Whereas the eleventh and twelfth centuries in the West had been on the whole an epoch of progress and deployment in all things of the mind and spirit, and the thirteenth one of maturity, consolidation and of relative equilibrium, the fourteenth was one of disruption, dissolution and revolution. In the century between Dante, seemingly a mature genius and one escaping from the limitations of his age, and Joan of Arc, a medieval figure whose career and outlook were as far removed from the modern world as those of St Anselm or

St Bernard, Europe had in fact passed through a process of change in which many of the aims and ideals of the previous age had been abandoned, and many of the ways of thought and dynamic ideas of the sixteenth century had been conceived. Among these changes a principal one was a retreat in the universities from metaphysics and what is called natural religion, and an abandonment of the attempt, which had reached a peak of endeavour with St Thomas Aquinas, to integrate philosophy and theology, reasoned conclusions and revealed truth. Whatever may have been the aim or precise achievement of William of Ockham, his predecessors and his successors, a principal consequence of his teaching and that of his followers was to discredit the claims of the human reason to make pronouncements upon the nature of God or the human soul, and to remove all limits to the absolute freedom of the divine will.

Whether or not this flight from metaphysics to formal logic, which has, at least to a superficial observer, so great a resemblance to the trend of philosophical thought in the two decades that have just ended, was directly influential in turning men's minds to a mystical approach to the mysteries of the faith is a question that cannot be answered by an historian. The true mystic, as we shall see our mystics asserting, is taught and led of God, not of man, and if any direct preparatory teaching helped to prepare minds for a mystical outlook, it was not the teaching of Ockham but the re-introduction of Neoplatonic and Dionysian ways of thought. Nevertheless it is noteworthy that, outside the sphere of influence of the universities, the literature of the day, and particularly the vernacular literature, has an inward-looking character recognizable in works of the most varied scope. Not only the author of *The Cloud* and Walter Hilton, but William Langland and the author of *The Pearl* (to take only the most eminent examples), move in the same world of ideas and motives. It is a world in which personal, individual problems and values are supreme, a world in which the kinds and degrees of love, divine and human, are matters of earnest debate, together with a search for clarity of conscience and a pity for those outside the visible Church, and a balancing of the claims of the lives of Martha and Mary, the active and the contemplative. It is a world quite different from the monastic world of the twelfth century, and from the pietistic, moralistic world of the later fifteenth century in the Netherlands. It is perhaps worth remembering that precisely in this century the number of Charterhouses in England begins to grow after a century that had seen no new foundation. In the sixty years between 1340 and 1400 no less than six of the nine English houses of the order came into being. True, the total population of all these new foundations, lay brothers included, was only a minimal fraction of the population of the country; it cannot greatly have exceeded one hundred souls; but in spiritual, as in aesthetic, creations it is the peaks, the highest attainments, that count and that give a character to a period or to a society, and not only the cloistered monks, but the bishops and magnates who founded the houses show by their choice of order what was most in esteem in their day. Neither Charterhouses nor movements of ideas can of themselves produce mystics, but it can at least be said that the religious climate of the age was sympathetic to a personal and "mystical" approach to the way of perfection; the older conception of the monastic life as the only secure way of salvation, the ark in the flood, had lost its wide appeal and its place had been taken, for earnest seekers, by the way of personal, if not solitary, endeavour. Similarly, with the breakdown of the vast theological synthesis, the way of truth might be shown in a more concrete form by the seer—a Catherine of Sweden, a Bridget of Sweden or a Julian of Norwich—or found for himself by the solitary contemplative.

If we turn now to the framework and character of the Church of the fourteenth century we shall find indications of a similar kind. The century-and-a-half that elapsed between the Norman Conquest and the Fourth Council of the Lateran (1215), which so nearly coincided in date with Magna Carta and the deaths of Pope Innocent III and King John, was, for England as for the Western Church in general, one of rapid development and increasing centralization upon the Roman Curia. Within this period the reformed papacy and the allied Gregorian reform of the Church in discipline and morals gradually extended and intensified their influence over the countries of western Europe, and though the strong moral force of the movement declined in mid-century the results in every department of church life were far-reaching and lasting. To take only two examples: the new religious orders, and the reformed branches of older institutes, invaded and filled England with abbeys and priories; at the same time the new canon law drew the whole Church into a closely woven network with Rome as the only source of law and the only court of appeal. Though the last decades of the twelfth century were a time of temporary confusion, the strands were drawn together more closely than ever by the genius of Innocent III, and his work was crowned by the great reforming council. During the whole of this period in England literacy, and the composition of literary works, was restricted in practice to clerks and above all to the monks and canons. The inspiration of the Gregorian reform had been monastic in origin, and the spiritual teaching and practices recommended had been monastic in character. It was an age in which all higher education and culture was one and the same throughout western Europe, and in which all literature was composed in Latin and was consequently steeped in the traditions, monastic and ecclesiastical, that had been accumulating since the age of St Augustine seven hundred years earlier. With very few exceptions, all spiritual instruction was given by monks and intended for monks, and only differed according to the specific competence or needs of the writer and the recipient, monk or nun, cenobite or hermit or ancress. The doctrine given had been formalized by centuries of use and was traditional and general in form. It dealt, that is to say, with large general principles, common to all devout men and women, and it lacked the personal touch, the urgency and the immediacy, that had characterized the instructions of the Fathers of the desert and was later to characterize those of the saints of the Counter-Reformation. Speaking generally, therefore, the vocal part of the Church in England, the only members who could and did express their thoughts and aims, were the bishops and higher dignitaries and the monks and other religious persons; in other words, those following the regular life of an approved institute. St Bernard's intimate revelation of his own spiritual experience in the later Sermons on the Canticle had no parallel in England and the only individuals addressed as such by spiritual writers were the ancresses to whom St Ailred and others directed their teaching, which usually took the form of a directory, rather than of practical instruction for prayer and the acquisition of the virtues.

The Fourth Council of the Lateran, summing up the practice and current teaching of the Church of the twelfth century, laid down a number of precepts for bishops, religious and layfolk. The century that followed, in England and in several other countries, was the great century of organization and of the evangelization of the people, both in the towns and in the country. The bishops amplified and staffed their cathedrals, organized parishes, instituted vicarages, visited their clergy and legislated for them and for their flocks. The friars, newly arrived, fervent and popular, preached and confessed the townspeople and the villagers.

At the universities both friars and secular clerks absorbed the comprehensive schemes of theology and canon law that a succession of compilers had prepared for the schools. Altogether, the thirteenth century was the epoch in which the parish and cathedral life of England was fully established under a hierarchy that was in the main learned and efficient and devout. In no other medieval century were there so many hard-working bishops devoted to the spiritual welfare of their dioceses. Nevertheless, though the age saw the beginning of a revival in the use of the vernacular in sermons and conferences, Latin still held the field for academic discussions and for philosophical, theological and other learned work, while French in its Anglo-Norman form was the medium used for much of the legal work and for the devotional and instructional treatises directed to the devout layman and laywoman.

In the fourteenth century a great change began. Treatises and prayer-books written in Latin and French were translated into English, and the vernacular was used increasingly for original work. The early translators at the turn of the century were followed by the English writings in prose and verse of Richard Rolle and others, and these in their turn by the magnificent flowering of Middle English in the works of Langland and Chaucer. England, indeed, did not stand alone in this linguistic change and in the appearance of a mature vernacular literature. France, with the *chansons de geste* in the north and the poets of courtly love in the south, Germany with its cycles of lays and legends, and above all Italy, with the rapid rise of the native tongue to the heights of elaborate poetic achievement in Dante, had preceded her. But it was a distinctive note of the first great decades of Middle English literature that the writings were intensely personal and were directed for the most part either to unknown individuals or to the lower levels of the literate public. Here the closest parallel is with Rhineland Germany, where the earliest vernacular prose is the copious sermon literature and the biographical collections of the German mystics. While the historian cannot give reasons for the appearance of saints or mystics, he can at least say that the emergence of a large literate class outside the ranks of the clerks and religious orders made it possible for the first time for a master to instruct his disciple, and for the mystic to describe his own experiences, in the simplicity, not yet formalized or conventionalized, of the vernacular language. Certainly, in the realm of spiritual direction the four writers whose works are described in the chapters that follow are unsurpassed in their use of words by those of any nationality in an age of great mystical and spiritual teachers.

Finally, the age was the first in which we catch a glimpse in our fellow-countrymen of those characteristics of language and mind which we recognize as English. They are no longer concealed behind the formalities of Latin or French. Just as the inhabitants of Langland's hovels and taverns, and the characters who exchange words in the prologues and connecting links of Chaucer's *Canterbury Tales*, are racy of the soil of England, so the author of *The Cloud*, Walter Hilton and Julian of Norwich speak a language and show personalities that we can feel to be English, and the counsel that they give can be, and is, as valid for us as for those for whom it was first intended. If Chaucer and Langland are the first great poets of our tongue, Rolle, *The Cloud* and Hilton show the first examples of great English prose.

Chapter IV

RICHARD ROLLE

THE earliest of the writers with whom we have to do is Richard Rolle. Rolle was by far the most widely known of the English mystics in the later Middle Ages, and he has again become familiar to readers in recent years. His medieval popularity was doubtless in part a result of the reputation for sanctity which persisted long after his death, and his modern celebrity has been partly due to his significance as a pioneer in the writing of English, but the primary reason at all times for his fame has been the number and variety of his works. Among the genuine writings are at least seven treatises in Latin, a dozen commentaries and translations of books of Scripture, in both Latin and English, eight letters and shorter pieces in English, and a number of English lyrics, and almost all these pieces are preserved in so many manuscripts, representing various traditions and various recensions, that the task of an editor is both laborious and unrewarding. In addition, Rolle's fame as a writer was such that he received the tribute of the ascription of numerous other works which, floating about in anonymous copies, were fathered upon him without apparent reason. At least eleven Latin works and fifteen English are ascribed to him in one or more medieval manuscripts; among these are writings now recognized as belonging to St Anselm, Suso, St Bonaventure and St Edmund of Canterbury. Even Hilton's *Scale of Perfection* has been reckoned as his, and he has only recently been deprived of the credit of writing the extraordinarily popular English treatise known as *The Prick of Conscience*. Fortunately.

the task of establishing the canon of Rolle's works by critical methods has been accomplished, on the whole very successfully, by Miss H. E. Allen, and the reader and critic can have fair confidence in his use of the documents.[1] Here we are interested primarily in Rolle as a mystic, and although it has been said with some truth that the mystical element is so ubiquitous as to be the most reliable of all the internal criteria of authenticity in his works, he is repetitive, his principles and ideas are relatively few, and usually expressed in terms of his own experience, so that there is little in the scattered allusions to the contemplative life that is not set out firmly and fully in two of his major works, the *Incendium Amoris*[2] and the *Melos Amoris*.[3]

Very little is known of Rolle's life, particularly in its later stages. This is not in itself surprising. The absence of biographical or autobiographical material concerning eminent men is as noteworthy in the fourteenth century as is its abundance in the twelfth. If we know little of Rolle, we have equally rare personal and biographical details of his great contemporaries William of Ockham and Thomas Bradwardine, and of such men of the next generation as John Wyclif, Walter Hilton and St John of Bridlington. It is, however, somewhat curious that the only source of detailed

[1] H. E. Allen, *Writings ascribed to Richard Rolle, hermit of Hampole, and materials for his biography*. New York and London (Oxford University Press), 1927. This vast work, replete with information of every kind on Rolle and his works, includes (pp. 430–526) an outline of his life, based on the researches of the author and other scholars. While the materials are extremely valuable, Miss Allen has a tendency to treat as acquired fact what she has previously put forward as a probable reconstruction.

[2] *Incendium Amoris*, ed. M. Deanesly (Manchester University Press), 1915. The Middle English translation by R. Misyn was printed by the Early English Text Society, original series no. 106 (1896). It has been turned into modern English as *The Fire of Love*, along with *The Mending of Life*, by F. M. Comper, London, 1914.

[3] *Melos Amoris*, ed. E. J. Arnould (Oxford: Basil Blackwell), 1957. The editor of this critical and very valuable edition defends *Melos* as the correct form of the title against the traditional *Melum*.

information of any kind is in the lessons composed in anticipation of his canonization, and that these should give the fullest detail of the early years.[4]

Richard Rolle was born at Thornton Dale, near Pickering, on the southern fringe of the moor south of the Cleveland Hills in the North Riding of Yorkshire.[5] He studied at Oxford, where he had as patron Thomas de Neville, son of the first Lord Raby, who enjoyed a prosperous career as a pluralist, ending his life archdeacon of Durham. There is no evidence of his taking a master's degree, and the indications are that he left Oxford after three or four years, at the age of nineteen or so, dissatisfied with the schools, and that almost immediately after his final return to the north he made a decisive break with the past[6] by leaving his father's house and adopting a hermit's dress and life. We are told that he entered a church, probably Pickering, and sat in the place usually occupied by the wife of John de Dalton, constable of Pickering Castle, and that he was recognized by her two sons, who had known him at Oxford. On the following day, the feast of the Assumption (15 August), he entered the pulpit and preached to a large congregation, which was duly impressed. It is a strange incident, for there is no evidence that Rolle was in orders of any kind, nor is there subsequent mention of any similar preaching. John de Dalton, who knew his father, took him home to dine and afterwards established him in a cell either in or near his manor, where he received subsistence for a time. From thence onwards, for the thirty-odd years of life that remained, scarcely anything is known of Rolle. He tells us that he was "persecuted" and left his original lodging, and we hear of clashes with monks and settlement in Richmondshire, and of a move thence to

---

[4] Printed as appendix V to *The York Breviary* (Surtees Society, vol. 75 ii, 1882), and translated by Comper, *The Fire of Love*, xlv–lviii.

[5] Allen, *Writings*, 431 ff.   [6] *Ibid.*, 449 ff.

Hampole near Doncaster. Practically nothing else is known of him save that a disciple, Margaret de Kirkby, a nun of Hampole, was enclosed as an ancress at Layton in Richmondshire in 1348, and that Rolle was then living twelve miles away. He died at Hampole, either on a visit or after another move, on 29 September, 1349, perhaps of the Black Death. Margaret de Kirkby, after a move to Anderby, returned to Hampole, where she probably lived in the cell near the convent occupied by her former director. He lived and died, it would seem, with the reputation of sanctity, and after some years reputed miracles took place at his tomb and elsewhere, and his body was "translated" into the priory church. There is no evidence that a formal attempt to secure canonization was ever made; if it was, it failed, though his younger contemporary and countryman, St John of Bridlington, a far less picturesque personage with no literary reputation, "made the grade" half a century later. Proceedings or expectations were at least advanced far enough for an unofficial office to be composed, and Rolle is sometimes referred to in manuscripts as St Richard.

Recent research has enabled us to see Rolle's career and personality in a clearer and firmer, if perhaps a less romantic, light than before. His alleged period of residence at the Sorbonne, which attracted and perplexed biographers for more than two decades, has been shown to be completely apocryphal,[7] and his supposed attack upon a bishop, with its

[7] Dom M. Noetinger, while preparing a French translation of the *Incendium*, (*Le Feu de L'Amour*, Tours, 1928), developed the opinion of Feret (*La Faculté de Théologie de Paris et ses Docteurs les plus célèbres*, iii 247–50) that Rolle had studied at the Sorbonne in an article in *The Month* (May, 1926). His conclusions were accepted by Miss Allen (*Writings*, 490 ff) and other writers on Rolle between 1926 and 1937, though all felt the great difficulty of fitting the episode into the framework of Rolle's life. The suggestion was conclusively shown to be a mare's nest by E. J. Arnould in an article in *Bulletin of the John Rylands Library* XXI i (April, 1937) reprinted in his edition of the *Melos Amoris*, Appendix II, 210–38.

subsequent repercussion upon his reputation, has been exposed as a complete misunderstanding of a sentence taken out of its context.[8] At the same time, a careful study of his sources, begun thirty years ago but still far from complete, shows him as a man of wide reading, not to say learning, in the traditional as well as the more recent authorities on the spiritual life. It is notable that, more than twenty years after he had left Oxford without (as it would seem) having done so much as complete his arts course, he was able to treat a controversial matter in the regular scholastic form of an "article" in a *Summa*,[9] and to know with accuracy the technical terms and accepted conclusions of the theologians and the writers of commentaries on the Scriptures. Though he was a poet of distinction, he was also much more than the lyrical nightingale of his own simile.[10] He could instruct and define with a sureness of touch that made him an unwelcome opponent, and it may well be that his greatest significance will ultimately be found, after his importance as an early master of English, in his achievement in instructing the educated and devout lay-folk and country clergy in matters of the ascetic and spiritual lives, and in the simple, vivid earnestness with which he drove home the meaning of the two great commandments of love. His commentaries on Job and the Psalms, and his English letters and treatises,[11] have a strength and firmness of doctrine that may surprise a reader familiar only with the more ardent, but also the more fluid, more mannered and even more extravagant individualism of the

[8] This alleged clash with authority in the person of a bishop (? of York), maintained by Miss Allen (*Writings*, 480 ff.), has been shown to rest upon a misunderstanding of a single phrase of Rolle's by E. J. Arnould, in an article in *Bulletin of the John Rylands Library* XXIII i (April, 1939) reprinted in *Melos Amoris*, Appendix I, 195–209.

[9] See article in last note (*Melos*, 197–8).

[10] *Incendium* ch. xlii, p. 277 (= *Fire of Love*, ed. Comper, II xii p. 190).

[11] Excellently edited by H. E. Allen, *English writings of Richard Rolle* (Oxford, 1931).

Incendium and of the *Melos*. Carl Horstmann, his first editor, may be pardoned for giving him the title of doctor of the English Church on the title-page of his first volume.[12] Rolle in this respect occupies a unique position. Whereas his predecessors and authorities, themselves regulars, had written almost exclusively for a cloistered *clientèle*, and those who came immediately after him, the author of *The Cloud* and Hilton, had a restricted, esoteric aim, and addressed the small *élite* of their contemporaries, Rolle wrote for his disciples, men and women, and for the devout wherever they might be, and when he wrote for a recluse it was to give general counsels of piety to one outside the regular life of a monastery. It was undoubtedly this general, easily grasped purpose, together with his use of the vernacular and the avoidance of the technical devotions of the cloister, that won and retained for his writings the esteem among all classes of the devout that they enjoyed from the day of his death till the extinction of the old ways and practices two hundred years later.[13]

What he may have gained as a figure of abiding significance in the history of English religious sentiment, Rolle has perhaps lost as a mystic. Here, undoubtedly, the claims that he makes for himself and for his experiences are too high; rather, perhaps, we should say that he fails altogether, through lack of experience and of knowledge, to reckon with the higher degrees of the mystical life. This failure was scarcely due to any fault of egoism on his part; he had never himself had a guide or received instruction; he was an autodidact both in his spiritual life and in his learning. He had found the monastic *ascèse* wanting, but he had little or no knowledge of the new message from the Rhineland, and had not heard

[12] C. Horstmann, *Yorkshire writers; Richard Rolle and his followers*, 2 vols. (London, 1895–6).
[13] Cf. A. G. Dickens, *Lollards and Protestants in the Diocese of York, 1509–38* (Oxford, 1959), 138–81, for the survival of Rolle in the sixteenth century.

the call to the heights that Tauler and Suso were even then uttering. In Rolle there is no trace of either Dionysian or Dominican influence. He was left to deal, as best he could, with the problems of his own time, and with the fashioning of his own life. He proceeded gropingly, and mistook the first glimpses of the life of contemplation for the plenitude of grace; he lacked the wise cautions that his successors were to multiply. Whether his "heat" and "song" were purely a release of subconscious activity, whether they were an unusually vivid and lasting "sensible devotion", or whether they were a psychological by-product or reaction of the natural powers to a real inflowing of grace we cannot tell. They were in any case, in technical mystical terminology, the experiences of a "beginner", and they do not seem to have altered or become more pure in the years that followed. As a mystic, Rolle has little or nothing to teach, and he was soon to be put into the shade, in the eyes of those best able to judge, by the author of *The Cloud*, who explicitly distrusted some of his practices and advice.[14] He remained, however, to instruct the devout and to encourage those who, like the Carthusian Methley almost two centuries later, had no strong spiritual guidance of their own.

Most of the passages dealing explicitly with the mystical life and with his own experiences occur in the two Latin treatises *Melos Contemplativorum* written probably *c.* 1330, and the *Incendium Amoris*, written probably ten or more years later, and it is in them that his conception of the contemplative life is to be sought. There is little evidence of development after the initial stages, which are recorded in the greatest detail fifteen or twenty years after the event, and the scanty references and assumptions of the later writings show no change or advance. It would seem that Rolle passed early, though not till some months or even years after his adoption

---

[14] See below, pp. 84, 96, 107–9.

of the hermit's way of life, through a moral and spiritual
crisis in which he overcame a passion for a woman, perhaps
a devout client, of his acquaintance,[15] and subsequently, after
an interval, experienced, in the order that he relates, the heat,
song and sweetness which remained with him intermittently
for as much of his life as we can see. He himself was clearly
persuaded that he had in no long time reached the highest
degree of contemplation, and in some of his earlier works
does not hesitate to say so.

In his early years as a hermit he felt the call to expose and
attack what seemed to him corruption in the Church of his
native region, and in particular the worldly life of the secular
clergy and the self-satisfied, mechanical piety of the monks.[16]
These attacks were either a cause or a consequence of persecution, or at least calumnies, directed against him by those who
were the objects of his criticism. His withdrawal from the
world had at first been only relative; he had lived in or near
the house of John de Dalton, and had later been supported
by other friends. It was only after a time that he became a
solitary in the strictest sense. Unfortunately, we know nothing of his circumstances for more than twenty years of his
later life, but his writings make it clear that he possessed, or
had access to, an adequate supply of books,[17] and, since he had
left Oxford so young and so long since, his very considerable
learning must have come from private reading. But though
he attacked the failings of priests, and extolled the solitary
life as against monastic ritualism, he is entirely orthodox, and
his thought moves wholly within the limits of the common

[15] For this, see Allen, *English Writings*, xxii–xxiii, where the relevant passage
from the *Encomium Nominis Jesu* is quoted. Cf. also *Melos Amoris* ed. Arnould,
xxiv, citing (note (a)) Rolle, *Canticles* f. 19.
[16] Especially in the *Judica me Deus* (Allen, *Writings*, 93 ff.).
[17] It was this "sound theological science and accuracy" (Noetinger, quoted
by Allen, *Writings*, 490) that helped to make the supposed sojourn in Paris a
plausible theory.

teaching of the Church. This is true also of his teaching on the contemplative life, where he follows closely the traditional presentation of St Augustine, St Gregory, Richard of St Victor and St Bonaventure. There is, however, a peculiar difficulty in setting out Rolle's pronouncements, for while he applies to contemplation all the traditional qualities, the "contemplation" he describes is neither the Augustinian nor the Dionysian nor the Taulerian "contemplation", but the heat, song and sweetness of his own experience, which to the mystical theologians of his own day and later ages would not be classed as contemplation in any sense of the word. In what follows, therefore, we may note the traditional phrases of Rolle while withholding our assent from their application to the spiritual experience of Rolle himself.

After his conversion and adoption of the hermit's dress Rolle would seem to have passed through a period of external and interior trials before the occurrence of what he ever after regarded as the first decisive moment in his spiritual growth. He relates this in full many years after; it is familiar, as it has been quoted by all who have written on Rolle, but no account is complete without it:

> When I was in the sour-sweet flower of youth, and the time had come of awakening to life, the grace of my Creator came to me . . . If I am to describe my progress I must tell of the life of solitude, for the Spirit breathing upon me directed my mind to pursue and to love this life, and henceforward I made it my care to lead it, so far as my weakness allowed. Nevertheless I remained among those who abounded with earthly riches, and I accepted food from them, and I heard the flatteries which have often drawn famous warriors from the heights to the depths. But I cast away such things in order to gain the one thing needful, and my soul was raised up to the Creator . . . From the beginning of the change of my life and mind until the opening of the door of heaven, so that the eye of my heart

might gaze upon heavenly things directly, and might see in what way to seek the Beloved and always long after him, three years, save three or four months, elapsed . . . While the door was still open, scarce a year went by before my heart felt in all reality the fire of eternal love . . . I was sitting in a certain chapel, and while I was taking pleasure in the delight of some prayer or meditation, I suddenly felt within me an unwonted and pleasant fire. When I had for long doubted whence it came, I learned by experience that it came from the Creator and not from creature, since I found it ever more pleasing and full of heat. Now from the beginning of that fiery warmth, inestimably sweet, till the infusion of the heavenly, spiritual harmony, the song of eternal praise, and the sweetness of unheard melody, which can be heard and experienced only by one who has received it, and who must be purified and separated from the earth, nine months and some weeks passed away.

For when I was sitting in the same chapel, and was reciting psalms as well as I might before supper, I heard above me the noise of harpers, or rather of singers. And when with all my heart I attended to heavenly things in prayer, I perceived within me, I know not how, a melody and a most delightful harmony from heaven, which abode in my mind. For my thought was straightway changed into a song, and even when praying and singing psalms I gave forth the selfsame sound. Thenceforth I broke out within my soul into singing what previously I had said, for abundance of sweetness, but in secret, for it must be in the presence of my Maker alone. I was not recognized by those who saw me, lest if they had known me they would have honoured me beyond measure, and so I would have lost part of the fairest flower and would have fallen into desolation. Meanwhile wonder seized me that I was taken up into such joy, and that God should have given me gifts which I knew not how to ask for, nor had thought that any, even the most holy, would receive such in this life. Certainly I think that this is granted to none as a thing merited, but freely to whom Christ has willed it. Yet I think that no one will receive it, unless he love specially the name of Jesus, and honour it so that he never allow it to fall from his memory save in sleep. He to whom this is given will, I think, achieve that other. So, from the beginning of my conversion to the highest degree of the love of Christ that I could attain by God's gift, the degree in which I sang the divine praises with joyful melody, was four years and about three months. This state, together with the former ones that prepared for it, remains to the end of my life. After death it shall be more perfect, because here the joy of love and the fire of charity begins, and in the heavenly kingdom it will receive most glorious consummation. And indeed he who is set upon these degrees or this life goes forward not a little, but does not rise to another state, nay rather, as it were confirmed in grace he is at peace so far as mortal man may be. Wherefore I long to return thanks and praises to God without ceasing.[18]

This long, carefully dated, and intimate narrative is Rolle's mystical *Summa*. Written, as it probably was, *c.* 1340, twenty years after his conversion,[19] it reflects his considered teaching, or rather, perhaps, his experience translated into general principles. Elsewhere in the *Fire of Love* he supplements what he tells in this place. Thus in the prologue he issues the warning that is almost common form among mystical writers:

Wherefore I offer this book for the consideration, not of philosophers, not of the wise of this world, not of great divines involved in endless questionings, but of the simple and un-learned, who endeavour to love God better rather than to know many things . . . For I think that what is contained here cannot be understood by those disputants who are expert in all knowledge, but inexpert in the love of Christ. So I intend to write not for them, unless they cast aside and forget all things

[18] *Incendium* xv, p. 187–90 (= *Fire of Love*, I xv pp. 69–72). The translation is mine. (D.K.)
[19] This would seem to represent the opinion of Arnould, *Melos*, lxv–lxvii, but other critics would favour an earlier date.

of the world and are on fire to be bound only by desire for the Creator.[20]

Further on he gives, again in phrases common to all the masters, the necessary conditions *sine qua non* of contemplation:

A man must be truly turned to him and in his innermost mind turned away from all visible things before he can experience the sweetness of divine love, even a little . . . for all love that is not devoted to God is evil, and renders evil those who have it . . . those who love worldly excellence with an evil love are inflamed with an evil passion and are further distant from the fire of divine love than is the distance between the highest heaven and the lowest place in the earth. They are indeed made like to their beloved, for they give way to worldly desire and holding fast to the old man take pleasure in the emptiness of visible life instead of truly happy love. . . . And indeed, as it is written, nothing is more evil than to love money, for while the love of any temporal thing fills the heart, it suffers him to have no inward devotion.[21]

Contemplation comes only to one who has been tried and purified:

Either in this life the fire of divine love will consume the rust of our sins and give charity to our souls . . . or after this life the fire of purgatory shall torture our souls, if it happen to us to escape the fires of hell, or if there be not in us a strength of love sufficient to purify us, we must be cleansed by tribulations, sicknesses and suffering. Oh good Jesus, scourge me here, pierce me here, strike me here, burn me here, that in the future I have no evil, but may feel thy love here and forever.[22]

[20] *Incendium*, prologue, p. 147 (= *Fire of Love*, I, i, p. 13).
[21] *Incendium*, ch. i, p. 148 (= *Fire of Love*, I, i, pp. 15–16).
[22] *Incendium*, ch. viii–ix, pp. 166, 168 (= *Fire of Love*, I, viii–ix, pp. 40, 43).

The beginner must practise severe discipline:

> First indeed it behoves a man to exercise himself unceasingly
> for many years in praying and meditating, scarcely taking the
> bare necessities for his body,[23]

and no one must expect a speedy growth:

> Certainly it is not to be supposed that anyone in the begin-
> ning of his conversion should reach the heights of contempla-
> tion or feel its sweetness, since it is well known that contem-
> plation is attained after much time and much labour, and not
> given straightway and broadcast to any who may come, for it
> is not within man's power to receive it, nor does a man's toil,
> however long he spend, merit it, but it is given of God's good-
> ness to his true lovers.[24]

Rolle describes elsewhere in what contemplation (as he calls
it) consists, but it must be remembered that he is always
descriptive, rarely analytic:

> Moreover in searching the scriptures as best I could I have
> found and realized that the highest love of Christ consists of
> three things—fire, song and sweetness. . . . I call that heat, when
> the mind is truly set on fire with divine love and the heart is felt
> similarly to burn with a love, not in imagination but really.
> For a heart turned into fire gives the feeling of the fire of love.
> Song I call it when now the sweetness of eternal praising is
> received in the soul with abundant heat, and thought is turned
> into song, and the mind dwells upon sweet melody. These two
> are not perceived in idleness, but in the height of devotion, and
> from them a third, that is inestimable sweetness is present.[25]

He insists that contemplation, like all other graces that
sanctify the soul, is not only itself a free gift of God, but is
also in its measures and times of bestowal hidden in the

[23] *Incendium*, ch. xxxii, p. 236 (= *Fire of Love*, II, ii, p. 136).
[24] *Incendium*, ch. xxxi, p. 234 (= *Fire of Love*, II, i, p. 134).
[25] *Incendium*, ch. xiv, pp. 184–5 (= *Fire of Love*, I, xiv, pp. 66–7).

mystery of predestination, and he writes with theological precision of spiritual graces in general:

> As in the house of God there are many mansions, and as in our fatherland there are diversities of reward in a single state of joy, some souls being more glorious, sublime, and nearer to God than others, so here below some are dear friends of Christ and some more dear . . . and each one of the elect is fittingly placed in his degree, nor can anyone go further than the degree to which the King has predestined him from eternity. When he reaches that place he is set in that degree, and even though he reach it by great labour, by much patience and suffering of tribulation, he is stablished in the degree to which he was chosen by the divine wisdom before he existed. And since the Creator has many sons whom he loves, what forbids it, what irks it, that because his Majesty loves some more than others he makes them more holy and raises them higher in the heavenly kingdom? [26]

This doctrine applies to contemplation, which for Rolle is the sanctifying grace *par excellence*:

> No man knoweth this gift save he who has received it; therefore they are few or none who tell of it. . . . All the clerks on earth may not imagine it or know what it is, but he that has it. . . . I say not that all shall attempt it [i.e. the heavenly song] but he to whom it is given, let him do what he wishes, for he is led by the Holy Ghost. [27]

It is God's free gift,

> But it is given soonest especially to those who have not lost that thing which is most pleasing to God by their way of living, that is, the flower of their youth. [28]

[26] *Melos*, ed. Arnould, xlix, p. 157.
[27] *Melos*, ed. Arnould, xxxix, note 42.
[28] "On Prayer" in *Minor Works*, ed. G. Hodgson, 151. Cf. St John of the Cross, *Spiritual Canticle*, stanza xxx (Peers, II, 352).

Rolle is throughout, as the titles of his two principal treatises imply, the prophet of Love:

> A reasonable soul cannot be without love while it is in this life . . . for to love and to be loved is the sweet business of all human life . . . if therefore you seek to be loved, love; for love demands its return. . . . Man's soul is sated with God alone; anything less than God cannot fill it. . . . I dare not say that all love is good for that love that is more delighted in creatures than in the Maker of all things, and sets the lust of earthly beauty before ghostly fairness, is ill and to be hated; for it turns from eternal love and turns to temporal that cannot last. Yet peradventure it shall be the less punished; for it desires and joys more to love and to be loved than to defile or be defiled.[29]

One other characteristic of Rolle remains to be noted. He shows himself in many of his writings uncommonly harsh in his judgment of women. Woman is the great danger to the spiritual man; she is the prime occasion of sin; she is deceitful, foolish, weak in her reason, beguiling; nothing is so dangerous and harmful as a woman's beauty, which she is always ready to exploit. This is perhaps the least attractive feature of Rolle's outlook, and it is not confined to a single work or to a short space of his life.[30] We know that he himself had to overcome an affection (which, according to his own account, was accompanied by a diabolical temptation) which would have ruined his spiritual life, but the woman in the case was ignorant of the whole affair, and the fault, if fault there was, lay at Rolle's door. In any case, Rolle in later life directed more than one woman, including Margaret de Kirkby, whom he treated with delicacy and affection, and whose devotion to him continued long after his death.

---

[29] *Incendium*, ch. xxiv, p. 210; ch. xxv, p. 214; ch. xi, p. 174; ch. xvii, pp. 195–6 (= *Fire of Love*, I, xxiv, p. 100; xxv, p. 106; xi, p. 52; xvii, pp. 79–80).
[30] See passages quoted by Arnould, *Melos*, xli–xlii.

Rolle is the first master of Middle English prose, and he can also be eloquent in Latin, but for the reader unfamiliar with the medieval vernacular the flavour of his style is apt to vanish in the process of modernization. The following extracts may show something of its variety:

Alas for shame, what can we, who are sinful and foul, say if we consider ourselves good, when they who are most clean and most love God consider themselves most sinful and most vile and most unworthy. . . . For, get who get may, this world is wide enough and good enough to win heaven in; and it is rich enough and pleasant enough and sinful enough to win hell with, flee who flee may. . . . Prayer freely beflowers our souls with blossoms of sweetness, with the fairness and sweetness of the fruit falling into hearts, which is freely to behold the fairness of God, in all meek virtues, lighting with the beams of his brightness all clean consciences and all meek hearts.[31]

When thou hast gathered home thine heart and its wits, and hast destroyed the things that might hinder thee from praying, and won to that devotion which God sends thee through his dear-worthy grace, quickly rise from thy bed at the bell-ringing: and if no bell be there, let the cock be thy bell: if there be neither cock nor bell, let God's love wake thee, for that most pleases God. And zeal, rooted in love, wakens before both cock and bell, and has washed her face with sweet love-tears; and her soul within has joy in God with devotion, and liking, and bidding him good-morning.[32]

Rolle had a very deep devotion to the Holy Name and to the Passion. Indeed, the Name of Jesus is to him a kind of talisman, and the frequent repetition an exercise in the presence of God. His long meditation on the Passion, which has often been printed[33] and quoted, though it is only a de-

[31] *Minor Works*, 153.   [32] *Form of Perfect Living*, ed. G. Hodgson, 116.
[33] Allen, *English Works*, 19 ff. Rolle probably made use of earlier writings when composing these meditations. Cf. "Meditations on the Passion ascribed to Richard Rolle", by M. M. Morgan in *Medium Aevum* XII 2 (1953), 93–103.

velopment of a theme found elsewhere, as in the *Ancren Riwle*, is perhaps the finest expression of that theme in English, and one of the best examples of Rolle's style. It is worth comparing this little treatise with the many similar meditations on the Passion which have been written since his day. Of the merely pictorial ones few, if any, are superior to his, for Rolle is always successful in avoiding false or strained sentiment, insignificant realism and far-fetched symbolism.

Rolle had many admirers and readers in the Middle Ages, and has found many friends among philologists and lovers of literature ever since his works began to be reprinted and his place in medieval thought and letters was vindicated by Carl Horstmann at the end of the last century. Much of Horstmann's praise was extravagant and ill-conceived, but Rolle's undoubted importance in the history of English prose, demonstrated so clearly by R. W. Chambers, together with his close correspondence with the romantic ideal of a medieval hermit and the beauty of some passages of his works, have attracted to him others besides professional scholars, and many of those who have written of him have accepted him also as a mystic of note. This is a mistake. Of purely mystical prayer and experience Rolle knows little or nothing. He is without question perfectly sincere in describing his experiences with their heat, sweetness and song, which seem to have continued at least for many years, but these, even if there is nothing of auto-suggestion about them, are physical and psychological phenomena common in a relatively elementary stage of the spiritual life, and as such are not found in those who have been raised to pure spiritual contemplation. In consequence, Rolle, as has been said, uses the term "contemplation" for a kind of prayer and spiritual experience considerably less advanced than that to which the author of *The Cloud* and Hilton, along with later mystical theologians, have rightly restricted it. His doctrine is in the main sound, but as it is based on common tradition interpreted in terms of his own very limited experience, it can be seriously misleading to the general reader if it is taken as a description of an advanced state of contemplative prayer. As a master, Rolle is far less reliable than *The Cloud* or Hilton and, as we shall see, both these writers are at some pains to counteract his influence on their disciples. Yet Rolle, both in the firm and clearcut instruction of his English letters, and in the eloquence of his most individual passages of autobiography, has an impressive and passionate sincerity:

In the beginning truly of my conversion and singular purpose I thought I would be like the little bird that languishes for the love of his beloved, but is gladdened in his longing when he that it loves comes, and sings with joy, and in its song also languishes, but in sweetness and heat. It is said that the nightingale is given to song and melody all night, that she may please him to whom she is joined. How mickle more should I sing with greatest sweetness to Christ my Jesu, that is spouse of my soul, through all this present life that is night in regard to the clearness to come, so that I should languish in longing and die for love.[34]

As the multitude of surviving manuscripts shows, Rolle was immensely popular in the two centuries between his death and the Reformation. He is found in company with the other mystics in the Charterhouses, at Syon and in some of the Benedictine abbeys, and his treatises circulated also among the clergy, gentry and townsfolk of the north, and are found in collections of books and wills. They also penetrated into Europe by three different channels: his commentaries on the psalms and Scripture were favourite reading with the Lol-

[34] *Incendium*, ch. xlii, p. 277 (= *Fire of Love*, II, xii, p. 190). Had Rolle himself heard the nightingale? Nottinghamshire nowadays would appear to be at the northern extreme of the bird's migration, but he may well have heard its song at Oxford.

lards, who added tendentious notes of their own, and several of these manuscripts found their way to Prague and elsewhere in Bohemia. Other works were left or given by English visitors to Switzerland and the Rhineland; others again passed by way of Syon to Vadstena in Sweden, while individual copies reached even Spain, Italy and France. In the early days of printing individual works appeared at Oxford, London, Paris and Cologne, and fuller collections were made by the Dominican Johann Faber at Cologne in 1535 and M. de la Bigne, reprinting Faber, in the same city in 1622. Thenceforward no attempt to present Rolle in fulness was attempted until the Early English Text Society began to publish him in 1866.

Chapter V

THE CLOUD OF UNKNOWING

WE have next to consider the writings of one who until recently had attracted less notice than Rolle, but who has some claims to be considered the most subtle and incisive, as well as the most original, spiritual writer in the English language. As his identity has yet to be established, he is usually known, from the title of his principal and most characteristic work, as the author of *The Cloud of Unknowing*, but three other pieces, two of them being translations, are certainly his, and three other short treatises may confidently be attributed to him both by reason of similarity of subject matter, style and language, and of their frequent association with the certainly authentic works in manuscript collections. These additional writings are *The Book of Privy Counselling*, *The Epistle of Prayer*, *The Epistle of Discretion*, the two translations of *Denis Hid Divinity* and *Benjamin Minor*, and the paraphrase of two sermons of St Bernard entitled *Of Discerning of Spirits*. Of the original works *The Book of Privy Counselling* is a continuation and companion of *The Cloud*, written considerably later and containing, both in style and matter, some of the writer's most mature and admirable work, while the two *Epistles* are shorter pieces bearing on the same themes and using the same ideas and expressions.[1]

[1] All previous editions have been antiquated by the critical texts of all the treatises by Professor Phyllis Hodgson, viz., *The Cloud of Unknowing* and *The Book of Privy Counselling* (Early English Text Society orig. ser. 218 (1944, reprinted with additions 1958) and *Deonise Hid Divinite and other treatises* (E.E.T.S. 231, 1955). For the general reader the best text of *The Cloud* and *The Book* (or *Epistle*) is that of Dom J. McCann, *The Cloud of Unknowing and other treatises*

Although sub-contemporary evidence and the number of manuscripts, in which the numerous variants and contaminations are proofs of a long and numerous ancestry, are alike witnesses of the immediate and lasting vogue which these treatises attained among religious and the devout, the identity of the author and the date and place of composition remain unknown. This is a remarkable fact, for we know that they attracted criticism and attention at once, and were familiar to subsequent writers, and it seems to show both that the author himself desired or welcomed anonymity, and that he was in a position which enabled him to secure it, even though all his writings were from the beginning directly intended for the benefit of all who might hope to profit by them. In any case, neither *The Cloud of Unknowing* nor any other treatise bears either in itself or in its manuscript tradition any precise indications as to the name, date, calling or dwelling-place of its author.

As regards his name, no single suggestion has yet been made which has even a reasonable degree of probability. Indeed, the only candidate with an arguable case is another of our mystics, Walter Hilton. The resemblances between the two in doctrine and language are certainly very striking and imply some kind of relationship. As one with unequalled knowledge of both has put it,[2] there are numerous phrases of both the unknown writer and of Hilton which might well be attributed to either by someone who knew both well, but had read neither recently. This close resemblance will appear even in the short groups of extracts given in this chapter and the next. Nevertheless, despite the advocacy of such competent critics as the late Abbot McCann and Miss Helen

(London: Burns Oates, 1924; 6 ed. revised 1952), which also contains (pp. 287 ff.) Fr Augustine Baker's valuable Commentary on *The Cloud*. References are given to the original edition.

[2] P. Hodgson, "Walter Hilton and *The Cloud of Unknowing*. A Problem of Authorship Reconsidered", in *Modern Language Review*, L, 1955.

Gardner,[3] the present writer is fully in accord with the editor of *The Cloud* and its companions when she pronounces decisively against this identification.[4] In addition to linguistic and stylistic difference, she points out that the two major works, *The Cloud* and *The Scale*, are each surrounded by a group of numerous satellites which recent scholarship is agreed in attributing to a common author. This circumstance, which of itself would go far to prove the existence of two clearly distinct agencies, would seem to make a common origin of all the pieces almost unthinkable, for it would make of Hilton the sole writer of more than a dozen works in Latin and English, and would leave him by far the most out-standing figure in Middle English prose literature. There are other powerful arguments against this identification. The scheme of the two works is wholly different: whereas *The Cloud* centres wholly upon what may be called a particular recipe of the spiritual life, *The Scale* deals with the whole of that life. Then, *The Scale* undoubtedly shows familiarity with *The Cloud*, but whereas *The Cloud* by preference con-siders the relations of the soul and God (i.e. the Godhead), in distinction to one of the Divine Persons, *The Scale* not only concentrates attention upon the Second Person, but alludes to Him even in His divinity as Jesus. Thirdly, and perhaps most significantly, whereas for the author of *The Cloud* the

[3] Dom J. McCann defended this identification, which Dom M. Noetinger favoured, in an article in the *Ampleforth Journal*, 1924. Miss Helen Gardner in the *Review of English Studies*, IX (April, 1933), 129–47, strongly opposed this view, but in her notice of Miss Hodgson's edition of *The Cloud* in *Medium Aevum*, XVI (1937), 36–42, she was inclined to consider it at least possible. In her earlier article she wrote (p. 147): "The two authors appear . . . to present strongly marked and different personalities, which no amount of common background or shared phraseology can disguise. Style, manner, vocabulary and imagery can be borrowed, but personality is inalienable." This was well said, but arguments of a more objective nature are not wanting, and have been provided by Miss Hodgson in her article "Walter Hilton and *The Cloud of Unknowing*" in *Modern Language Review*, L (1955), 395–406.
[4] E.g. *The Cloud*, pp. lxxxiv and 198 (note).

contemplative stands as it were between a cloud of forgetting (of creatures) and a cloud of unknowing (of God), the soul in *The Scale* enters into a night, which is, as with the active nights of St John of the Cross, the abandonment of all enjoyment and perception of creatures, and emerges therefrom into the light of God. Above all, there is the conviction, which almost all thoughtful readers must have experienced at one time or another, that they have encountered in the two books two minds and personalities that are wholly distinct the one from the other.[5]

As regards the date and place of writing, we are equally without precise information. The oldest extant manuscript dates from the early decades of the fifteenth century, but gives proof of being already far removed from the archetype. At the other limit, it is as certain as may be, short of demonstration, that the author knew Rolle's works, and that Hilton knew *The Cloud* fairly early in his own life as an author, say *c.* 1380 at latest. This would give a period between *c.* 1345 and 1386 as a *floruit*, and such slight linguistic and other indications as exist would favour the end rather than the beginning of this space of years for the writer's activity, which must itself have covered at least a decade or two. As for place, we have fairly firm linguistic evidence for an East Midland origin, that is, Nottinghamshire, Leicestershire and the adjacent parts of Lincolnshire and Northamptonshire, and this would accord well with Hilton's early acquaintance with *The Cloud* and the northern provenance of several of the manuscripts.[6]

Internal evidence as to the writer's identity is very slight. While we are probably justified in deducing his priesthood from the blessing with which he ends more than one of his

[5] This last sentence was written before reading the judgment of Miss Gardner, above, note 3.

[6] For all this see Miss Hodgson's learned introduction.

writings,[7] there is no trait or allusion that would suggest allegiance to any particular religious order, though more than one editor has given expression to a feeling that he had at some time or another spent years in a religious house. There is perhaps ground for taking one allusion to imply that he was a hermit or solitary.[8] He is certainly well read in relevant literature, and has more theological knowledge and precision than has Rolle, though his apparently technical phrases may come from some writer he is recalling. *The Cloud* is addressed to a young man of twenty-four, who is now in a "singular" or "solitary form of living", but who had previously been "a servant of the special servants [of God, where he had] learned to live more specially and more ghostly in His service".[9] This phrase, if taken as a precise description, would suit exactly the class of Carthusian *redditi*, and no other; at this period, the only Carthusian house in existence in the North Midlands was Beauvale, founded 1343.[10] This circumstance, however, would tell us nothing of the subsequent status of the young man, still less of that of his counsellor. After all our discussions, we must admit our ignorance, though there is no other medieval anonymity that we would more eagerly wish to dissolve. Thirty years ago, the present writer inclined to think of the author of *The Cloud* as a Carthusian, and not as a priest with a cure or title of any kind. Now he would be more disposed to imagine him as a solitary, perhaps an ex-religious and, if so, preferably a Dominican, such as the distinguished solitary at Lynn thirty years later who was among the counsellors of Margery Kempe.[11]

[7] E.g. *The Cloud* H (Hodgson) 133; M (McCann) ch. lxxv 175.

[8] *The Cloud* H 36/7; M ch. x p. 38.   [9] *The Cloud* H 14/5; M i 8.

[10] For the Carthusian *redditus* see E. M. Thompson, *The English Carthusians* (London, 1932), 123–4. Beauvale was the house in which Adam Horsley, Hilton's disciple, sought the habit.

[11] His clear dependence upon the Rhineland school of spirituality and his technically orthodox Thomism on the vexed and topical issue of grace (see below, pp. 93–5) are strong arguments to show Dominican associations.

When we turn from our search for a local habitation and a name for the author of *The Cloud* to consider his mental and spiritual characteristics, we are brought face to face with a very striking figure who is also the master of a very individual, racy, idiomatic prose style, with a gift for short and almost epigrammatic phrases of doctrine and counsel. As we shall see, though he is deeply versed in mystical literature, his debt to those he treats as his masters is often relatively small; he is a wise, confident, forceful counsellor with a single message which is at once traditional and his own, and which he delivers with an assurance that we feel must come from personal experience of what he preaches. *The Cloud* is the longest and most important of the works attributed to him, and there can be little doubt that it is also the earliest. It has all the air of being an early programmatic writing, containing what may be felt to be novel teaching. Stylistically, also, it is somewhat less fluent, and it has a vein of apologetic and one or two curiously crude passages[12] which are without parallel in the other books. Of these *The Book of Privy Counselling* may well be the latest. In it the writer refers to *The Cloud*, to the translations of Denis and Richard of St Victor, and to the *Epistle of Prayer*,[13] and both the last-named and the three short English treatises give an impression of mature wisdom and assurance, and cover a wider range of spiritual experience and counsel, than does *The Cloud*.

Whereas Rolle shows relatively little literary and doctrinal background in his mystical passages and is individual in style and approach rather than in his ideas and the instruction that he gives, the author of *The Cloud*, while revealing a wide acquaintance with several well-known authorities, and a respect for their words, is nevertheless profoundly original

---

[12] E.g. that on necromancy in *The Cloud*, ch. lv, and perhaps also that on idiosyncrasies in ch. liii.

[13] *PC* (*Book/Epistle of Privy Counsel*) H 154/15–18; M vii 211.

in the sense that no other, either before or after, sets out exactly the same instructions with the same points of emphasis. His editors, and in particular Abbot McCann and Professor Hodgson, have done much to indicate where his debt principally lies.[14] Richard of St Victor is closely followed in two long passages and many shorter, where the writer shows familiarity with both the *Benjamins*; St Augustine's teaching on the active and contemplative lives is embodied at some length, as are other points of doctrine of Augustine and Gregory the Great; the *Scala Claustralium* of Prior Guigo II of the Grande Chartreuse, and the instruction for novices written by Hugh of St Victor are likewise laid under contribution. The source *par excellence* of his method is, however, the pseudo-Denis, and in particular the *Theologia Mystica*. This short treatise was, as we have seen, translated by the author of *The Cloud*, and he himself writes:

> Truly, whoso will look in Denis's books, he shall find that his words will clearly confirm all that I have said or shall say, from the beginning of this treatise to the end.[15]

This, however, is not precisely true. In the first place, no one in his position and indeed no medieval scholar or theologian of any kind could have grasped the outlook and meaning of the Syrian monk of the early sixth century. Those who read him, with implicit trust in his sub-apostolic authority, transformed his teaching into something compatible with their own theological and spiritual background. Next, the author of *The Cloud* did not read Denis in the original Greek, but in two medieval Latin translations, those of Johannes Sarracenus (d. 1160) and Thomas Gallus (d. 1240), assisted by the latter's commentary.[16] Gallus, abbot of

---

[14] H lvii–lxxxii; M xv ff.   [15] H 125/13–15; M lxx 164.
[16] Hodgson, introd. lxii ff. Cf. "An Unknown Commentary of·Thomas Gallus on the pseudo-Dionysian Letters", in *Dominican Studies*, 1948, by Fr D. Callus, O.P.

St Andrew's, Vercelli, and a canon of the Victorine order, had displayed even more than the customary medieval skill in noiselessly adapting a work of ancient thought to medieval conditions, and had made love rather than understanding the characteristic occupation of the contemplative, thus rendering Denis viable among Thomists and Bonaventurans. The author of *The Cloud* follows Gallus in this respect and elsewhere also; whatever may have been his sincere belief that he was following Denis, his doctrine is something quite other than that of *Hid Divinity*. The latter is primarily an intellectual progress, in which grace and unreformed human nature may be assumed, but are certainly not explicitly admitted, and the end is an intellectual union, while *The Cloud*, for all the apparently esoteric quality of some of its instructions, is in fact a manual of traditional ascetic and mystical teaching, based on current orthodox theology and assuming the customary sacramental and devotional life of medieval England.

Many years ago, in an article dealing with *The Cloud*, the opinion was put forward that a (hitherto unidentified) master had inspired the English writer.[17] Since that day, two scholars have suggested possible candidates for this position of authority. Fr James Walsh, S.J., in a doctoral thesis presented in the Gregorian University at Rome,[18] has analysed and illustrated the teaching of Thomas Gallus with many references to *The Cloud*, and Professor Phyllis Hodgson[19] has called attention to the similarities between the well-known medieval treatise *De adhaerendo Deo* and the doctrine of the English mystic. That the theories and instructions of these

[17] M. D. Knowles, "The Excellence of *The Cloud*", in *Downside Review*, LII (1934), p. 81. "The persuasion remains that there is a source of *The Cloud*, if only a great and inspiring teacher, whose name we shall never know."

[18] "*Sapientia Christianorum*." *The doctrines of Thomas Gallus Abbot of Vercelli on contemplation* (Rome, 1957). Fr Walsh has kindly allowed me to read and use this unpublished thesis, which it is hoped will in time see the light in print in some form.

[19] P. Hodgson, *The Cloud*, introd.

two writers bear strong resemblance to those expounded by the author of *The Cloud* cannot be denied: the crucial question is, whether the relationship is that of derivation or of similarity only.

In the case of Thomas Gallus it had been shown by Dom J. McCann, before Fr Walsh began his researches, that his was the version of Dionysius upon which the author of *The Cloud* had principally drawn. Fr Walsh, in his valuable and penetrating study, shows many points of verbal and doctrinal resemblance, and establishes beyond a doubt that Thomas Gallus was a mystical theologican of power and originality, who transmitted, if he did not also propound, a body of teaching which influenced St Thomas Aquinas and became part of the common heritage of Catholic mystical theology. At the same time, it is not evident that the abbot of Vercelli inspired what are the peculiar characteristics of *The Cloud* and its companions: the insistence on the blind, "naked" act of loving attention; the clear distinction between the human and the supernatural "modes" of the theological virtues, the insistence on the sharp line between natural and supernatural knowledge, and the incommunicability and the imperceptibility to the natural powers of the light of contemplation. Likewise, there is no hint in Thomas Gallus of the abundant and shrewd practical advice of *The Cloud*. In other words, while the influence of Gallus is very real, it is not the specifying influence.

With the treatise *De adhaerendo Deo* the case is different.[20] Here the resemblances are within the specific realm of practical instruction, while at the same time the difficulties of supposing derivation are external but insuperable. The *De adhaerendo Deo* was traditionally ascribed to St Albert, and though this has been widely questioned it had been con-

[20] The treatise is printed in the last vol. of the works of St Albert and has often been printed separately.

sidered at least as coming from his school. More than thirty
years ago, however, Martin Grabmann showed from manuscript evidence that the work as we know it was composed
by the Benedictine abbot John of Kastl *c.* 1410.[21] His decision
has been challenged, and it would seem at least certain that
Kastl's work was that of a compiler rather than that of an
original thinker, but the late date of the existing text makes
it impossible to regard the treatise as in any direct sense a
source of *The Cloud.* Moreover, when closely regarded,
Kastl appears to draw upon the teaching of Cassian as frequently as upon that of Dionysius; there is no cloud of unknowing and little discussion of the relations between natural
and supernatural, and the treatise lacks the deeper mystical
experience of the *Epistle of Prayer.* The emphasis throughout
is on concentration rather than on loving. It is undoubtedly,
however, a collateral relation, and this of itself goes far to
show (if evidence were needed) that the author of *The Cloud*
stands in the Rhineland tradition. Indeed, the researches of Fr
Walsh and Miss Hodgson, even if neither has succeeded in
isolating an "only begetter" of the English mystic's doctrine,
have between them confirmed previous suggestions as to his
ancestry, and when to Gallus and the Rhineland we add the
undoubted influence of Thomist theology, the achievement
of blending these elements into a new doctrinal synthesis and
practical instruction is perhaps not beyond the powers of a
single spiritual genius.

It may well be that some of the teaching, if not the actual
reportage of the sermons of Tauler had come to England by
the agency of members of his order. Certainly the author of
The Cloud, who has often and without great discrimination
been acclaimed as the first English spiritual writer to follow
Dionysius, is the first to reflect some, at least, of the characteristic features of the Dominican school of the Rhineland,

[21] M. Grabmann, *Mittelalterliches Geistesleben,* I (1926), 489–524.

and in particular the insistence upon naked faith, the restriction of the highest and purest contemplation to an incommunicable and indescribable experience without any external manifestations, and the treatment of contemplation as a prolongation of the normal Christian life of grace.

We may now endeavour to set out, largely in his own words, the teaching of the unknown master. Once and for all, it must be emphasized that he is addressing a specified individual (and, by extension, others of similar gifts and needs) who is seeking advice as to his conduct on entering upon and pursuing a life of solitude and contemplative prayer. He gives this advice first and foremost by prescribing a single practice or exercise, which in itself is almost a way of life, and which the disciple is to maintain, so far as grace and his condition will allow, always and in all places:

> Lift up thine heart unto God with a meek stirring of love, and mean himself and none of his goods. And thereto look that thou loathe to think on aught but himself, so that nought work in thy mind nor in thy will but only himself. And do that in thee is to forget all the creatures that ever God made and the works of them, so that thy thought or thy desire be not directed or stretched to any of them, neither in general nor in special. . . . At the first time when thou dost it, thou findest but a darkness and as it were a cloud of unknowing, thou knowest not what, saving that thou feelest in thy will a naked intent unto God . . . this darkness and this cloud . . . hindereth thee, so that thou mayest neither see him clearly by light of understanding in thy reason, nor feel him in sweetness of love in thy affection. And therefore shape thee to bide in this darkness as long as thou mayest, evermore crying after him whom thou lovest. For if ever thou shalt see him or feel him as it may be here, it must always be in this cloud and in this darkness. . . . Smite upon that thick cloud of unknowing with a sharp dart of longing love.[22]

[22] *The Cloud* H 16/3–26/12; M iii 11–12 vi 24.

These instructions are remarkably similar to those inculcated time and again, and in all his writings, by St John of the Cross:

> He that would attain to being joined in a union with God must not walk by understanding, neither lean upon experience or feeling or imagination, but he must believe in His Being, which is not perceptible to the understanding, neither to the desire nor to the imagination nor to any other sense, neither can it be known in this life at all . . . and thus a soul must pass beyond everything to unknowing.[23]

And again:

> The will remains loving that which is certain, in very truth, by the light of faith, being empty and in darkness, with respect to its feelings, and transcending above all that it can perceive with its understanding and with its own intelligence, believing and loving beyond all that it can understand.[24]

Three points may be noted in this teaching. The first is, that it is addressed only to those in whom the requisite vocation and ascetical preparation are found; the second, that it is primarily an exercise of the will, of the love of God; and thirdly, that it rests upon the theological (or metaphysical) assumption, that between the soul and God there is always a "cloud of unknowing", the Dionysian *caligo ignorantiae*.

The first point is essential, but it may easily be overlooked, for it is enunciated on the first page of the prologue, and not again. His instructions, the writer says, are to be read only by "such a one as doth all that in him is, and hath done long time before, for to able him to contemplative living, by the virtuous means of active living. For else it accordeth nothing to him."[25] What the signs are that may reassure him of his

[23] *Ascent of Mount Carmel*, II iv (Peers, 1933, I, 75).
[24] *Letter XI* to a religious (Peers, III, 280).
[25] *The Cloud* H 1/12–2/8; M 3–4.

call are set out at a much later stage, but the prologue, which clearly was written last of all, gives a cross-reference.

The second point is equally important. It is the great, indispensable, but probably unconscious modification that the commentator of the thirteenth century made when adopting Denis. He transferred to him what he had learnt from the theologians of the West. As the author of *The Cloud* has it:

> To the knowing power [of man] God is evermore incomprehensible, but to the . . . loving power he is, in every man diversely, all comprehensible to the full.[26] . . . For why, love may reach to God in this life, but not knowing[27] . . . And therefore she [*sc.* the Magdalen] hung up her love in this cloud of unknowing, and learned to love a thing the which she might not see clearly in this life by light of understanding in her reason.[28]

Here he is at one with the Thomist and other theologians, who teach that whereas in knowing the object known is present in the knower in a manner reduced to his capacity, in loving the lover goes out of himself to attain his object as it is in itself.

The third point is the most characteristic of all. The writer tells us that there is between the faculties of the soul and God a cloud of unknowing, and that the task of the would-be contemplative is to thrust all created things under a cloud of forgetting, and to beat with love upon the cloud of unknowing:

> This travail is all in treading down of the thought of all the creatures that ever God made, and in holding of them under

[26] *The Cloud* H 19/4; M iv 15.   [27] *The Cloud* H 33/11; M viii 33.
[28] *The Cloud* H 46/15; M xvi 52. Cf. St John of the Cross, *Ascent*, II, v (Peers, I, 82). "The preparation of the soul for this union is not that it should understand or perceive or feel anything concerning God . . . but that it should have purity and love." Letter XI (III, 280): "It is through the operation [of the will] that it becomes united with God, and has its end in Him who is love."

the cloud of forgetting . . . this is man's travail with the help of grace.[29]

Gradually, however, as the cloud of forgetting becomes established, the love changes in character:

[and the other travail], the stirring of love, that is the work of only God. And therefore do on thy work, and surely I promise thee he shall not fail in his.[30]

We may again compare St John of the Cross:

When the soul voids itself of all things and achieves emptiness and surrender of them (which, as we have said, is the part the soul can play) it is impossible, if the soul does as much as in it lies, that God should fail to perform His own part by communicating Himself to the soul, at least secretly and in silence.[31] It is more impossible than that the sun should fail to shine in a serene and unclouded sky.

In this process, the consciousness of self and all its faults and imperfections, and of its "otherness" to God—in other words, the self-knowledge demanded by so many spiritual writers as a necessary condition of advance—cannot be

---

[29] *The Cloud* H 61/22; M xxvi 73.   [30] *Ibid.*

[31] *Living Flame*, stanza III, §46 (Peers, III, 185). Both this and the passage from *The Cloud* are following Eckhardt; cf. *Sermon II* on the Eternal Birth: "When he [God] finds you ready, he must act, and pour into you, just as when the air is clear and pure, the sun must pour into it and may not hold back. Surely it would be a very great defect in God if he did not do a great work, and anoint you with great good, once he found you empty and innocent." Cf. Tauler, *Sermons* (trans. Elliott, Washington, 1910), p. 120: "It would be attributing a grave fault to God to suppose that he would not do his great work in thee, as soon as he finds thee capable of receiving it. It is more impossible than that the sun should fail to shine in a serene and unclouded sky." Cf. also *Ascent*, II xv (Peers, I, 129, §4). Eckhardt and Tauler, neoplatonizing, fail to emphasize the absolute gratuity of the grace of contemplation; St John follows them in a passage not typical of his doctrine, but in his case the context supplies the necessary caution.

exorcized without a special grace of sorrow and self-despisal:

> When thou hast forgotten all other creatures . . . there shall remain betwixt thee and thy God a naked knowing and a feeling of thine own being; the which knowing and feeling must always be destroyed, ere the time be that thou mayest feel verily the perfection of this work . . . without a full special grace full freely given by God, and also a full according ableness on thy part to receive this grace, this naked feeling and knowing of thy being may in no wise be destroyed. And this ableness is nought else but a strong and a deep ghostly sorrow . . . this sorrow and this desire [*sc.* to lack the feeling of his being] must every soul have and feel in himself as God vouchsafeth to teach his ghostly disciples according to his good will and their according ableness . . . ere the time be that they may perfectly be oned unto God in perfect charity.[32]

As the soul grows more pure its prayer becomes purer:

> And look that nothing remain in thy working mind but a naked intent stretching unto God, not clothed in any special thought of God in himself, how he is in himself, or in any of his works, but only that he is as he is. This naked intent, freely fostered and grounded in very belief, shall be nought else to thy thought but a naked thought and a blind feeling of thy own being . . . Think no further of thyself than I bid thee do of thy God, so that thou be one with him in spirit . . . For he is thy being, and in him thou art what thou art, not only by cause and by being, but also he is in thee both thy cause and thy being. . . . Bear up thy sick self as thou art unto gracious God as he is . . . in lustiness of love to be knitted and oned in grace and in spirit to the precious Being of God in himself only as he is, without more.[33]

[32] *The Cloud* H 82/23–85/8; M xliii 104–7. Cf. St John, *Dark Night*, II, vi (Peers, I, 407): "And when the soul is indeed assailed by this divine light, its pain, which results from its impurity, is immense; because, when this pure light assails it, in order to expel its impurity, the soul feels itself to be so impure and miserable."   [33] *PC* H 135/19–139/14; M i 180–1 ii 186.

Finally, the reasoning and imaginative faculties cease to trouble the soul:

> And well is this work likened to a sleep. For as in a sleep the use of the bodily wits is ceased, that the body may take his full rest in feeding and strengthening of the bodily nature: right so in this ghostly sleep the wanton questions of the wild ghostly wits and all imaginative reasons be fast bound and utterly voided, so that the silly [= "poor"] soul may softly sleep and rest in the lovely beholding of God as he is, in full feeding and strengthening of the ghostly nature.[34]

In these passages, the writer has clearly been describing the transition from ordinary, "active" prayer to something higher, through what has been labelled diversely at one time or another the "prayer of simplicity", "abandonment", "loving regard" and "acquired contemplation" to the beginnings of the "prayer of quiet" as described among others by St Teresa. It is scarcely necessary to note that there is no trace of "quietism" in the teaching of *The Cloud*. The "sleep of the faculties" refers only to the external activity; within the soul, intellect and will are receiving:

> Know thou right well . . . that although I bid thee thus plainly and thus boldly set thee to this work, nevertheless yet I feel verily . . . that Almighty God with his grace must always be the chief stirrer or worker, either with means or without, and thou only . . . but the consenter and sufferer.[35]

He explains the difference between this prayer in its developed contemplative form and that of the ordinary devout Christian with great theological accuracy:

> It is the work of God only, specially wrought in whatever soul he liketh, without any merit of the same soul . . . and yet he giveth not this grace, nor worketh this work, in a soul that

[34] *PC* H 152/3; M vi 207.   [35] *PC* H 155/5-11; M vii 212.

is unable thereto . . . God giveth it freely without desert. The condition of this work [= contemplation] is such that the presence thereof enableth a soul to have it and to feel it. And that ableness may no soul have without it. . . . Let it be the worker, and thou but the sufferer; it sufficeth unto thee that thou feelest thyself stirred sweetly with a thing thou knowest never what, except that in this stirring thou hast no special thought of anything under God, and that thine intent be nakedly directed unto God . . . In this work men shall use no means, and men may not come thereto by means.[36]

We may once again compare St John of the Cross:

When it comes to pass that the soul is conscious of being led into silence, and hearkens, it must forget even the practice of that loving advertence of which I have spoken, so that it may remain free for that which the Lord then desires of it. . . . I will raise up my mind above all the operations and all the knowledge that can be comprehended by my senses, and above that which they can keep and retain within themselves: all this I will leave below . . . so that through contemplation I may receive that which is communicated to me from God. For we have already said that pure contemplation consists in receiving.[37]

The author of *The Cloud* bases his explanation fully and firmly upon the evangelical teaching:

Our Lord is not only porter himself, but also the door . . . whoso entereth not by this door . . . he is not only a night thief, but a day skulker.[38]

For

Truly without him it is nought that we do, himself saying: "Sine me nihil potestis facere." That is . . . without me first principally stirring and principally moving, and ye only but

[36] *The Cloud* H 69/2-7/18; M xxxiv 83, 85-6.
[37] St John, *Living Flame*, III, §§35-6 (Peers, III, 179-80). The last sentence is axiomatic for the whole doctrinal position of the saint.
[38] *PC* H 159/5-160/8; M ix 218, 220.

consenting and suffering, ye may do nothing that is perfectly pleasing to me . . . in things active, man's learning and his natural knowledge shall principally abound as in working, God graciously consenting . . . but in things contemplative the highest wisdom that may be in man is far put under, so that God be the principal in working, and man but only consenter and sufferer. . . . In actives he must be either with suffering or with consent, or else with both . . . in contemplatives by principal working, asking of them nothing else but only sufferance and their consent.[39]

He knows well enough of the existence of divine communications which are other than "pure contemplation", and also of the imperfect way in which they may be received by the mind, or reflected by the imagination and senses. In the passage that follows we may see an assertion of traditional teaching, but we may also feel that the writer has Rolle and his school in mind:

[Sometimes God] will inflame the body of a devout servant of his . . . with full wonderful sweetness and comforts. Of the which, some be not coming from without into the body by the windows of the wits, but from within, rising and springing from abundance of ghostly gladness, and from true devotion of spirit. Such a comfort and such a sweetness shall not be held suspect and (shortly to say) I trow that he that feeleth it may not hold it suspect. But all other comforts, sounds and gladness and sweetness that come from without suddenly . . . I pray thee have them suspect. . . . And therefore I pray thee to lean listily to this meek stirring of love in thine heart and follow thereafter . . . such a good will is the substance of perfection. All sweetness and comforts, bodily or ghostly, be to this but as it were accidents . . . lean not too much on them . . . for peradventure thou mayest be stirred to love God for the sake of them . . . some creatures be so weak and tender in spirit, that unless they were somewhat comforted by feeling of such sweet-

[39] PC H 162/8–163/18; M x 223–5.

ness they might in nowise abide nor bear the diversity of temptations and tribulations . . . and there be some creatures so strong in spirit . . . that they need not much to be fed with such sweet comforts in bodily feeling.[40]

At a higher degree of spiritual experience he begins to make the distinction between rapture and ecstasy and pure contemplation that was finally clarified by the Spanish Carmelites:

Some think this matter so hard and so fearful that they say that it may not be come to without much strong travail coming before, nor conceived but seldom, and that but in time of ravishing [he is perhaps here thinking of a version of the teaching of St Augustine and St Gregory]. . . . I answer that it is all at the ordinance and the disposition of God, according to their ableness in soul . . . for some there be that without much and long ghostly exercise may not come thereto, and yet it shall be but full seldom and in special calling of Our Lord that they shall feel the perfection of this work: the which calling is called ravishing. And some there be that be so subtle in grace and in spirit, and so homely with God in this grace of contemplation, that they may have it when they will in the common state of man's soul . . . and have full deliberation of all their wits bodily and ghostly, and may use them if they desire; not without some difficulty, but without great difficulty.[41]

And he adds, again nearly anticipating the teaching of St John:

All the revelations that ever saw any man here in bodily likeness in this life, they have ghostly meanings. And I trow that if they unto whom they were showed had been so ghostly, or could have conceived their meanings ghostly, that then they had never been showed bodily.[42]

[40] *The Cloud* H 90/20–94/17; M xlviii 115–1120. For a fuller discussion of these points, see article by the present writer, "The excellence of *The Cloud of Unknowing*" in *Downside Review*, LII (Jan., 1934), 71–92.
[41] *The Cloud* H 125/24–126/16; M lxxi 165–6.   [42] H 107/11–15; M lvii 138.

We may compare St John:

> Let it be believed, too, that if Our Lord were not about to
> lead the soul in a way befitting its own nature . . . He would
> never communicate to it the abundance of His Spirit through
> these aqueducts, which are so narrow . . . the soul must not
> allow its eyes to rest upon that outer husk . . . and in this way
> the soul takes from these things only that which God intends
> and wills, namely, the spirit of devotion, . . . and casts aside
> that which He would not give if these gifts could be received
> in the spirit without it, namely the apprehension of the senses.[43]

The similarity between the doctrine of *The Cloud* and *The
Book* and that of St John of the Cross has already been noted.
It is very remarkable, and may be considered in three points
in particular: first, the teaching that contemplation, though
an eminent grace, is in the normal line of development in the
growth of the soul towards perfection; secondly, the insistence that all purely natural activities and satisfactions of
mind and will must cease before the supernatural mode of
action can begin, and that this supernatural manner of acting
is imperceptible to the natural powers and cannot be expressed by them, all apparent perceptions being "accidental"
overflowings into the faculties; thirdly, the assertion of the
purgative nature of the darkness of contemplation, with the
consequent two "passive nights" of sense and spirit. We may
take these three points in order.

The words from the prologue have already been quoted in
part, where the author says he is writing only for

> such a one as hath in a true will and by a whole intent purposed
> him to be a perfect follower of Christ. And that not only in
> active living, but also in the sovereignest point of contemplative
> living, the which is possible by grace to be come to in this
> present life by a perfect soul.[44]

[43] *Ascent of Mount Carmel*, II, xvii (Peers, I, 143–4).   [44] See above, note 25.

Likewise, he says of his disciple that he has been drawn by God from the "common degree" of Christian man's living to the "special degree" (i.e. the religious life) and now to the third degree (i.e. the contemplative) which is on the way to "that degree of living that is perfect". And, like St John, he expressly identifies this life with the gospel teaching:

> In this work thou art learned to forsake the world and to despise it. And—that more is—in this thou art learned to forsake and despise thine own self, according to the teaching of Christ in the gospel, saying thus: "Whoso will come after me, let him forsake himself."[45]

St John's constant teaching, that the natural, active manner of working of mind and will is in contemplation superseded by the supernatural mode is at the root of all his practical instructions. Failure to appreciate this caused many writers—Father Baker, as we shall see, among them—to lose their way in the subject. The active night of the author of *The Cloud* is as thorough as that of St John.

> Do that in thee is to forget all the creatures that ever God made and the works of them, so that thy thought or desire be not directed or stretched to any of them, neither in general nor in special.[46]

And again:

> I except not one creature, whether they be bodily creatures or ghostly. . . . But to speak shortly, all should be hid under the cloud of forgetting. . . . Yea . . . in this work it profiteth little or nought to think on the kindness or the worthiness of God, nor on our Lady, nor on the saints or angels in heaven, nor yet on the joys of heaven.[47]

---

[45] *PC* H 154/21; M vii 211.   [46] *The Cloud* H 16/6; M iii 11.
[47] *Ibid.*, H 24/11–25/7; M v 21–2.

The reason is that all such thoughts are

> a sharp and clear beholding of thy natural wit, printed in thy reason within thy soul. And where thou askest me whether it be good or evil: I say that it must always be good in its nature; for it is a beam of the likeness of God.... But in the higher part of contemplative life, a man is above himself and under his God ... And all the while that the soul dwelleth in this deadly body, evermore is the sharpness of our understanding in beholding of all ghostly things, but most specially of God, mingled with some manner of fantasy.[48]

As with the intellect, so with the will:

> While our desire is mingled with any manner of bodilyness —as it is when we stress and strain us in spirit and body together—so long is it farther from God than it should be if it were done ... in soberness and in purity and in depth of spirit.[49]

Further still, and with a clear distinction of sense and spirit and a suggestion of the doctrine, developed so fully by the great theologian John of St Thomas, that the special Gift of Understanding separates natural from supernatural, and God from creatures, by making clear what is not God and what is not supernatural:

> [Our outward bodily wits] be ordained that with them men should have knowing of all outward bodily things, and in nowise by them come to the knowing of ghostly things. I mean by their works [i.e. by what their exercise attains to]. By their failings we may ... be verily certified that those things be ghostly things and not bodily things. In this same manner it fareth within in our ghostly wits when we travail about the knowing of God himself. For have a man never so much ghostly understanding in knowing of all made ghostly things, yet may he never by the work of his understanding come to the knowing of an unmade ghostly thing: the which is nought but God.

[48] *Ibid.*, H 30/3–33/15; M viii 29, 33.   [49] *Ibid.*, H 89/6; M xlvii 113.

But by the failing he may. Because that thing he faileth in is nothing else but only God.[50]

In other words, what is essentially supernatural cannot fall within the cognizance of the natural powers except *à rebours*:

> Thou mayest neither see him [God] clearly by light of understanding in thy reason, nor feel him in sweetness of love in thine affection.[51]

As for the "night of the soul", the author explains his "darkness" as St John does his "night":

> When I say darkness, I mean a lack of knowing [and feeling]: as all thing that thou knowest not, or hast forgotten, is dark to thee; for thou seest it not with thy ghostly eye.[52]

The "active nights" of sense and spirit are the subject of almost all the two treatises we are considering. They are clearly distinguished in a chapter heading:

> That right as by the failing of our bodily wits we begin most readily to come to the knowledge of ghostly things, so by the failing of our ghostly wits we begin most readily to come to the knowledge of God.[53]

The author is also clear, with St John, that the apparent darkness is caused by the excess of infused light:

> A soul is more blinded in feeling of it [*sc.* this nought] for abundance of ghostly light, than for any darkness or wanting of bodily light.[54]

He is also clear as to the purifying force of the darkness:

> Thou thyself art cleansed and made virtuous by no work so much,[55]

[50] *Ibid.*, H 124/17; M lxx 163–4.   [51] *Ibid.*, H 17/4; M iii 12.
[52] *Ibid.*, H 23/20; M iv 20.
[53] This is the chapter-heading to ch. lxx of *The Cloud*; M, p. 162; not in H.
[54] *The Cloud* H 122/11; M lxviii 160.   [55] *The Cloud* H 16/15; M iii 12.

and therefore:

> Suffer meekly the pain.... For truly it is thy purgatory. And
> then when thy pain is all passed ... it is no doubt to me that
> thou art cleansed ... from sin.[56]

And more fully:

> Wonderfully is a man's affection changed in the ghostly feel-
> ing of this nought [i.e. the cloud of unknowing]. For at the
> first time that a soul looketh thereupon, he shall find all the
> special deeds of sin that ever he did since he was born, bodily
> or ghostly, privily and darkly printed thereupon ... until the
> time be that with much hard travail and many bitter weepings
> he have in great part washed them away. Sometimes in this
> travail he thinketh that to look thereupon is to look as on hell;
> for he thinketh that he despaireth to win to perfection of ghostly
> rest out of that pain. Thus far inwards come many; but for
> greatness of pain that they feel and for lacking of comfort they
> go back to the consideration of bodily things ... he that
> abideth feeleth some comfort and hath some hope of perfection
> ... nevertheless ever he feeleth pain ... and therefore he calleth
> it nought else but purgatory.[57]

And in another place:

> Now art thou in the ghostly sea shipping over from
> bodiliness into ghostliness. Many great storms and temptations
> shall rise in this time and thou knowest never whither to run

[56] *The Cloud* H 67/21; M xxxiii 82.
[57] *The Cloud* H 122/18–123/15; M lxix 160–1. M (with some MSS) reads in
last line "nought else but purgatory"; H (with other MSS) "not hell but purgatory". For the thought cf. St John, *Dark Night*, II, vi (Peers, I, 412): "At
times ... the soul seems to be seeing hell and perdition opened ... for here on
earth they are purged in the same manner as there, since this purgation is that
which would have to be accomplished there." *Living Flame*, II, §§25, 27 (Peers,
III, 152–3): "For even as impure spirits ... pass through the pains of fire in the
life to come, even so ... these souls must pass through the fire of these said
pains here below ... And there are many ... when it pleases God to begin to
bring them through the first trials ... who are unwilling to pass through them,
and flee away."

for sorrow—and all this he doth because he will have thee
made as pliant to his will ghostly as a Roan glove is to thy
hand bodily ... for know thou right well, that though God
sometimes withdraw these sensible sweetnesses, these fervent
feelings, and these flaming desires, nevertheless he withdraweth
never the rather his grace in his chosen ... for grace in itself
is so pure, so high, and so ghostly, that it may not be felt in our
sensible part ... and in this time is thy love both chaste and
perfect.[58]

It is inevitable that those accustomed to the categories, now
classical, of St John of the Cross should ask themselves to
which of the two nights these descriptions refer. The answer
is not easy. Mystical theologians, in this respect not unlike
psychologists, are sometimes misled into regarding the current classifications of their science as clear-cut and unchange-
able as the parts of a machine. Actually, as the great masters
themselves remind us, the divisions of the life of grace and the
spirit, though resting upon real psychological and theological
entities and powers, are in their external manifestations re-
fracted and clouded by all the differing circumstances,
qualities and graces of the individual soul. St John himself remarks upon the innumerable variations of quality and dura-
tion of the two nights, and notes that the night of sense, in
particular, may vary between an almost imperceptible state
of aridity and a long and severe period of trial resembling
the night of the spirit. Nevertheless, if there is to be any distinction made between the two nights the soul must be regarded as essentially removed from the bondage of sense and
imagination by the first night (of sense), and if this is so, and
if the author of *The Cloud* is using words aright, the two extracts given above can refer only to the passive night of sense,
albeit to an unusually severe form of that night.

If this is so, then it must follow that he does not (contrary

[58] PC H 167/14–169/24; M xii 231–5.

to what some commentators have maintained) describe the heights of contemplation that follow the night of spirit, and in fact no passage in his writings can be shown to do so. The following is probably his highest flight of mystical description:

> In this time it is that thou both seest thy God and thy love, and nakedly feelest him also by ghostly oneing to his love in the sovereign point of thy spirit, as he is in himself, but blindly as it may be here, utterly spoiled of thyself and nakedly clothed in himself, as he is, unclothed and not lapped in any of these sensible feelings, be they never so sweet nor so holy, that may fall in this life. But in purity of spirit properly and perfectly he is perceived and felt in himself as he is, far removed from any fantasy or false opinion that may fall in this life.[59]

This might at first be thought to represent the experience of a soul that had passed through the night of the spirit, but it must be remembered that the transformation of the soul is a gradual progress from light to light. St John in the following passage is speaking of the early stages of the mystical life:

> For thus [sc., by abandoning "meditation"] little by little and very quickly, divine calm and peace will be infused into his soul, together with a wondrous and sublime knowledge of God, enfolded in divine love.[60]

A remarkable feature of *The Cloud* is the author's clear and consistent scheme of the workings of grace. We have seen that he separates contemplatives from the "common" and "special" degrees among Christians, but he is clear that the grace of contemplation is a development of sanctifying grace, though its mode of action is different:

> In things active, man's learning and his natural knowledge shall principally abound as in working, with God graciously

[59] PC H 169/17-26; M xii 234-5.
[60] St John of the Cross, *Ascent*, II, xv (Peers, I, 129).

consenting ... but in things contemplative, the highest wisdom that may be in man, as man, is put far under, so that God be the principal in working, and man but only consenter and sufferer.[61]

He continues:

In all our doings, lawful and unlawful, active and contemplative, without him we may do nothing. He is with us in sin only by sufferance and not by consent ... in deeds that be active and lawful, he is with us both by suffering and consent ... in deeds that be contemplative, he is with us principally stirring and working, and we only but suffering and consenting.[62]

He returns to the subject later in words that anticipate very closely more than one page of St John:

A travail shall he have ... and that a full great travail, unless he have a more special [i.e. unusual] grace. ... But, I pray thee, wherein shall that travail be? Surely not in that devout stirring of love that is continually wrought in his will, not by himself, but by the hand of Almighty God, who is evermore ready to work this work in every soul that is disposed thereto, and that doth what in him is, and hath done long time before, to enable him to do this work. But ... this travail is all in treading down of the thought of all the creatures that ever God made ... for this is man's travail, with the help of grace. And the other above—that is to say, the stirring of love—that is the work of only God.[63]

[61] *PC* H 163/5–11; M x 224–5.
[62] *PC* H 163/18–25; M x 225. Cf. St Thomas, Ia, IIae, 1, iii, a. 2: "In illo effectu in quo mens nostra est mota et non movens, solus autem Deus movens, operatio Deo attribuitur, et secundum hoc dicitur gratia operans." Also IIa, IIae, 1. 52, a. 2, ad 1: "In donis Spiritus Sancti mens humana non se habet ut movens, sed magis ut mota."
[63] *The Cloud* H 61/12–62/2; M xxvi 72–3. Cf. St John of the Cross, *Living Flame*, III, §46 (Peers, III, 185): "Let them [*sc.* directors] strive to disencumber the soul and to set it in a state of rest ... it is this that the soul must do as far as in it lies, as the Son of God counsels, in these words: He that renounceth not all the things that he possesseth cannot be my disciple."

If we look more closely still we shall see that he distinguishes with great care between the different species of grace, between operating and co-operating grace (*gratia operans, co-operans*), between grace that stirs and grace that assists (*gratia excitans, adjuvans*) and between graces external to the will itself, whether creatures used by God as instruments, or illuminations and persuasions given to the mind by God, and the actual movement of the will by grace that later Thomism knew by the name of "physical premotion":

> For know thou right well . . . that although I bid thee thus plainly and thus boldly set thee to this work, nevertheless yet I feel verily without error or doubt that Almighty God with his grace must always be the chief stirrer [*excitans*] and worker [*adjuvans*], either with means [external grace] or without [internal grace], and thou only the consenter and sufferer [*gratia operans*].[64]

Finally, when reassuring his disciple that no evil spirit can move his will, he analyses still further the interior movement of the will by God, giving with great precision the doctrine of St Thomas:

> Trust then steadfastly that it is only God that stirreth thy will and thy desire, plainly by himself, without means either on his part[65] or on thine.[66] And be not afraid of the devil, for he may not come so near. He may never come to stir a man's will, except occasionally by means and from afar [e.g. by putting imaginations into the mind, not by stirring the will], be he never so subtle a devil. For sufficiently and without means[67] may no good angel stir thy will: nor, shortly to say, anything

[64] *PC* 155/5-11; M vii 212.

[65] In technical theological language, God is said to work in us *immediatione virtutis et suppositi*.

[66] Again in technical language God is said to work *in potentia liberi arbitrii*, i.e. not merely attracting the will by illuminating the intellect. And God alone can do this.

[67] In theological language: *efficaciter immediatione virtutis et suppositi*.

but only God. So that thou mayest here by these words understand somewhat—but much more clearly by experience—[68]
that in this work men shall use no means [i.e. holy imaginations
or natural efforts] and that men may not come thereto with
means.[69]

This doctrine of grace has been stressed, and those unfamiliar
with the history of the schools in the fourteenth century
might well think it to have been overstressed, but in fact it is
extremely significant. From the beginning of the century onwards, the conception of grace as a real entity had been
gradually losing ground under the attacks of the new school
of thinkers. This traditional conception of grace as a quality
of the soul, strictly and truly the beginning, the seed, of
eternal life, had vanished under the attacks of the followers of
Ockham (who in this matter was not himself in intention a
revolutionary), and had become a relationship, an attitude
towards God, not necessarily implying any new principle or
quality or spring of action in the soul concerned. Grace was
simply a right relationship of man towards God consequent
upon God's acceptation of man's love.[70] By the middle of the
century there was no sort of agreement in academic circles
in England as to the nature of grace; not even the Dominicans
held as a body to the traditional opinion. It is therefore very
noteworthy that the author of *The Cloud* holds throughout
to the Thomist position without any hesitation. It is difficult
to suppose that anyone outside the Dominican order would
have kept so closely to the teaching of Aquinas, and if we
look for a Dominican school of theology teaching orthodox

[68] Cf. St Teresa, *Life*, xv, 6. "A person of experience . . . cannot possibly fail
to understand at once that it is not a thing that can be acquired." Also *Relation*,
VIII, §3. "This will be easily understood by him whom Our Lord shall have
raised to this state: but by him whom He has not, not."

[69] *The Cloud* H 70/23–71/8; M xxxiv 86.

[70] For this, see the present writer's "The censured propositions of Uthred of
Boldon", in *Proc. of the British Academy*, xxxvii (1951), 305–42, and G. Leff,
Bradwardine and the Pelagians (Cambridge, 1957), ch. viii.

Thomism round about 1350, we can find it only in the Rhineland.

The author of *The Cloud* never mentions Rolle, either directly or by implication, but there are one or two passages where he would seem to be warning his hearers against dangers that might come from his teaching. Thus he writes of those who substitute bodily for spiritual travail and

> merit to have their breasts either inflamed with an unnatural heat, caused by misruling their bodies . . . or else they conceive a false heat wrought by the fiend . . . and yet peradventure they ween that it is the fire of love, gotten and kindled by the grace and the goodness of the Holy Ghost.[71]

Similarly he warns them:

> all other comforts, sounds and gladness and sweetness, that come from without suddenly and thou knowest never whence, I pray thee have them suspect.[72]

We shall see that Hilton is still more emphatic and pointed in his warnings.

Some space has of necessity been devoted to the critical and doctrinal aspects of *The Cloud* and its companion treatises, but it would be unpardonable to leave this writer and master without some notice of his characteristics as a person and as a literary artist. No careful or sympathetic reader can fail to appreciate the depth and power of his exposition, or the range of his style, which passes from homely instance to piercing theological clarity without an effort. We may instance his instructions on the treatment of distractions:

> When thou feelest that thou mayest in nowise put them down, cower then down under them as a caitiff and a coward overcome in battle, and think that it is but folly to strive any longer with them, and therefore thou yieldest thyself to God in the hands

[71] *The Cloud* H 86/5–14; M xlv 109.   [72] *Ibid.*, H 91/4; M xlviii 116.

of thine enemies . . . and this meekness meriteth to have God himself mightily descending, to venge thee of thine enemies, so as to take thee up and cherishingly dry thy ghostly eyes, as the father doth his child that is on point to perish under the mouths of wild swine or mad biting bears.[73]

Or his explanation of the power of short prayer:

A man or a woman, affrighted by any sudden chance of fire, or of a man's death, or whatever else it be, suddenly in the height of his spirit he is driven in haste and in need to cry or to pray for help. Yea, how? Surely not in many words, nor yet in one word of two syllables. And why is that? Because he thinketh it over long tarrying, for to declare the need and the work of his spirit. And therefore he bursteth up hideously with a great spirit, and cryeth but one little word of one syllable: such as is this word FIRE or this word OUT.[74]

Or his eloquent defence of liberty of spirit:

For silence is not God, nor speaking is not God; fasting is not God, nor eating is not God; onliness is not God, nor company is not God, nor yet any of all the other such two contraries. He is hid betwixt them, and may not be found by any work of the soul, but only by love of thine heart. He may not be known by reason. He may not be thought, gotten nor traced by understanding. But he may be loved and chosen with the true, lovely will of thine heart. Choose thee him.[75]

And, finally, he is the master of the simple, arresting phrase and clause:

Take good, gracious God as he is, plat and plain as a plaster, and lay it to thy sick self as thou art. Or, if I shall say otherwise, bear up thy sick self as thou art and try for to touch by

---

[73] *Ibid.*, H 66/23–67/14; M xxxii 80–1.
[74] *Ibid.*, H 74/14–22; M xxxvii 92–3. "Out" here is an interjection; cf. "out upon him!"
[75] *A Pistle of Discrecioun of Stirings* (in Hodgson, *Deonise hid divinite*), 71/19–26.

desire good, gracious God as he is. . . . Step up then stoutly and taste of that treacle.[76]

Such a blind shot with the sharp dart of longing love may never fail of the prick which is God.[77]

For virtue is nought else but an ordered and a measured affection, plainly directed unto God for himself. . . . As thus, for example, may be seen in one virtue or two instead of all the other; and well may these two virtues be meekness and charity. For whoso might get these two clearly, he needeth no more; for why, he hath all.[78]

And if a man will but see written in the gospel the wonderful and special love that our Lord had to her [Mary Magdalen] . . . he shall find that our Lord might not suffer any man or woman —yea, not her own sister—to speak a word against her, but that he answered for her himself. Yea, and what more? He blamed Simon the Leper in his own house, because he thought against her. This was great love: this was surpassing love. And this I say in confusion of their error who say that it is not lawful for men to set them to serve God in contemplative life, except they be secure beforehand of their bodily necessaries. For they say that "God sendeth the cow, but not by the horn". And truly they say wrong of God, as they well know.[79]

Most moving of all, perhaps, are the words with which *The Cloud of Unknowing* ends:

For not what thou art, nor what thou hast been, seeth God with his merciful eyes, but what thou wouldst be.[80]

The Cloud and its companions are indeed a notable landmark in English spiritual literature. They are the first and

---

[76] *PC* 138/28–139/7; M ii 186.   [77] *Pistle of Discrecioun*, 72/12.

[78] *The Cloud* H 39/17–24; M xii 42–3.

[79] *The Cloud* H 56/3–57/11; M xxii 65–xxiii 67. "God sendeth the cow, etc.", a medieval version of "God helps those who help themselves", was current throughout Europe at least two centuries before *The Cloud*. The author may have taken it from Guigo, *Scala Claustralium*, ch. xii: "Et ita [Deus] quasi prodigus [donorum], ut vulgo dici solet, bovem cornu trahit, quando non vocatus se infundit."

[80] *The Cloud* H 132/19; M lxxv 175.

last example of an English master basing himself avowedly upon the pseudo-Denis. But, as we have seen, the dependence upon Denis is essentially small. The real significance of *The Cloud* is that it is the earliest instance in any vernacular literature of a direct, practical, non-schematic instruction in the entrance and progress in the contemplative life understood (as it has been ever since) as the life of mystical, infused prayer. From the day of its appearance to the present time it has been found, wherever it has been known, an eminently practical book for the class of reader (a very small one) to which it was originally addressed. In the later medieval centuries it was prized among Carthusians and recluses, including the last generation of the London Charterhouse, and it was with them that it went overseas, and there came into the hands of Father Augustine Baker, who used it as a manual for the young community of Cambrai, to which he was chaplain. His words may serve as a fitting end to this chapter:

> I esteem it to be an excellent book, for those that understand it, and for everyone that reads it, so far as he understands it and doth not pretend to understand more of it than indeed he doth.[81]

[81] *The Cloud*, ed. McCann, p. 292.

58905

Chapter VI

WALTER HILTON

THE distinguished and nameless author of *The Cloud* was followed, within a very few years, by a spiritual writer of different temper but of equal distinction, and with a very similar outlook upon the life of the spirit. When reading *The Cloud* and its companion treatises we feel the impact of a strong, original, masterful and independent personality; Hilton is gentler and less aloof. Although no one without very deep and varied spiritual experience could have written *The Scale of Perfection*, we do not feel when we are reading it that we are listening to a record of personal striving, any more than we do when we read the *Imitation of Christ* or the *Introduction à la vie dévote*. We think rather of the wisdom and holiness of the writer's spirit, and of the care that has gone to the moulding of his work.[1] *The Cloud* and the *Book of Privy Counselling* follow no ascertainable scheme or order of topics, the thought eddies and returns, and though the *Book* appears to be written by a man of greater spiritual maturity than is perceptible in *The Cloud*, it is by no means certain that the writer is treating of another and a higher degree of the contemplative life. *The Scale*, on the other hand, though not composed as a single treatise, and

[1] The most sensitive appreciation of Hilton is perhaps that of Miss Helen Gardner, "Walter Hilton and the mystical tradition in England", in *Essays and Studies* (English Association), XXII (1937), 103–27; see also Professor R. M. Wilson, "Three Middle English Mystics", in *Essays and Studies*, new series ix (1956); Dom G. Sitwell in *Downside Review*, LXVII–LXVIII (1949–50) and *Clergy Review*, June, 1959, and Miss J. Russell-Smith in *The Month*, no. 208 (Sept., 1959), 133–48, and "Walter Hilton and a Tract in Defence of the Veneration of Images", in *Dominican Studies*, VII (1954).

not without its share of medieval digression and disorder, is a methodical work, the outcome of deliberate planning, with a beginning and an end.

Though much useful work has been done upon Hilton's writings in the past twenty years, a critical edition of *The Scale* is still wanting,[2] and there has been no recent and comprehensive discussion of the known facts and dates of his life, and of the authenticity of the various works ascribed to him. As, however, the only one of these in which he appears as a mystical teacher is *The Scale*, we may, for present purposes, reserve our attention for this, his principal treatise.

Walter Hilton was long thought, on the authority of manuscript ascriptions, to have been a Carthusian, but it is now accepted that he was an Augustinian canon of the priory of Thurgarton in Nottinghamshire, and there is considerable manuscript evidence that he died on 24 March, 1396. The events of his earlier career, however, and the dates of his writings are still uncertain. Copyists of his manuscripts give him the title of Magister, which his theological knowledge does not belie, though it is not notably wider than that of the author of *The Cloud*, and he does not find a place in Mr Emden's biographical dictionary of Oxford men. Moreover, Miss Helen Gardner has recently produced evidence from Hilton's

[2] Several scholars (Mr S. S. Hussey, Fr T. P. Dunning, Miss C. Kirchberger, Miss J. Russell-Smith) are at present engaged in the heavy task of preparing a critical edition of *The Scale*, for which Miss R. Birts has done some preparatory work in an unpublished B.Litt. thesis. The only textual discussion in print is Miss H. Gardner's "The Text of *The Scale of Perfection*," in *Medium Aevum*, V (1936), 11–30. There are two good practical editions available, that of E. Underhill (1923, reprinted 1950) based upon selected MSS and slightly modernized, and that of Dom G. Sitwell (1953) based on the Underhill text but rewritten in current English. References above are given by page to this latter, as being probably easier to come by, but most of the extracts follow Miss Underhill's text (which has the same division of chapters) as giving somewhat more precisely the theological nuances of Hilton's thought, and page references are given to this text in brackets. The French translation by Dom M. Noetinger (Paris, 1923) has valuable notes and indications of the source-literature.

works *De Imagine Peccati* and the *Epistola Aurea* to show that when he wrote these works Hilton was himself a solitary.[3] As the *Epistola Aurea* was written to encourage one Adam Horsley to become a Carthusian, and as Horsley was Controller of the Great Roll as late as 1375, Hilton's entry into Thurgarton must have been later than that date, and his life as hermit must be placed between his career at the university and his religious profession. It is an unusual life-story, and the Austin canons at this time were not an austere, contemplative body, though it is worth remembering that a contemporary Austin canon, prior of Bridlington, was conspicuous for sanctity of life. In fact, Hilton is almost as shadowy a figure to us as is the author of *The Cloud* or as their two contemporaries of genius, William Langland and the author of *The Pearl*.[4]

The first part of *The Scale of Perfection*[5] was originally written, like *The Cloud* and much of Rolle, for the guidance of a single friend of the author, though, as is clear enough, Hilton was aware that his words would go further. This friend was apparently an ancress, though she is called a religious and was bound to the breviary and lived within the precinct of a monastery. She may well have been a nun who had proceeded to the stricter life of a solitary within her own conventual building. *The Scale* consists of two parts or books of almost equal length; the second is a development from the first, though not addressed to the same person, nor indeed to any particular individual, but editors are agreed (and readers will scarcely gainsay) that the second book has a

[3] H. Gardner, *Essays and Studies*, XXII, 108–13.

[4] There is no contemporary authority for the statement sometimes made that Hilton was prior of Thurgarton, and the dates of the known priors, if correctly transmitted, would eliminate the possibility. He is, however, referred to in a fifteenth-century MS as "canon and governor" of Thurgarton.

[5] The title seems to have been given after Hilton's death. The two parts have no direct connection with one another, and several MSS add a third part, *sc.* the *Mixed Life*, now printed among the minor works.

somewhat different and more advanced teaching which supposes a space of at least several years between them. If in the case of *The Cloud* the critical edition does little more than give a sound text amid a welter of insignificant variants, an edition of *The Scale* might well have great value for the student of Hilton's doctrine. Miss Underhill, now more than thirty years since, drew attention both to what she considered a significant change in expression between the two books and to traces of a later recension of a number of words and phrases. In her opinion, Hilton in Book I showed himself to be under the influence of the austere "theocentric" teaching of *The Cloud*, whereas in the second book a warmer, "Christocentric", piety was visible. She also noted that many passages, especially in the second book, had been rewritten with the name of Jesus replacing the name of God. She loyally added that some of the clearest instances of devotion to the Holy Name were to all appearances original, but the matter is obviously one of interest and can only be answered when a fully critical text has been constituted. The point was taken up by Miss Helen Gardner more than twenty years ago.[6] She showed conclusively that there was no manuscript evidence of a change of opinion or doctrinal revision on Hilton's part. The long passage on the Holy Name, omitted by numerous MSS, is unquestionably genuine, though it may have been written separately and later inserted in *The Scale*. As for the "Christocentric" passages noted by Miss Underhill, they are mostly words or phrases inserted later and often somewhat clumsily, possibly by Carthusian owners of *The Scale* influenced by the fifteenth-century pietistic writers of the order. Doubtless the matter will be treated fully by the editors of the forthcoming critical text. For the present all that can be said is that while there is no question of any doctrinal change between the two books, or

[6] In her article mentioned above, note 2, in *Medium Aevum*, V.

between *The Cloud* and Hilton—for both writers at all times insist that all grace comes to men through Jesus Christ and through His Gift of the Holy Spirit, it would seem that Hilton in his last years was in the habit of using the Holy Name of Jesus more frequently, not only in place of "Christ" in references to the sacred humanity, but also as a personal name for the Divine Son, where the author of *The Cloud* would have used the name of God.

While *The Cloud* and its companions are essentially monographs on a particular tract of the contemplative life, swollen with a number of digressions, long and short, *The Scale* is in aim a *Summa* of the whole spiritual life and an attempt to give in outline its degrees and duties. Hilton is in all things traditional and conservative, and ostensibly makes even more use than his predecessor of the Fathers such as Augustine and Gregory, and medieval writers such as Bonaventure and the Victorines,[7] but he is perhaps unconsciously almost as revolutionary as the author of *The Cloud* in his abandonment of arbitrary divisions of the soul and of allegorical interpretations of Scripture in favour of a homely and practical analysis of the devout life and of the ascetical preparation needed for one embarking upon a life tending towards spiritual perfection. *The Cloud*, the work of a dynamic personality, circles round a single magnetic focus; *The Scale*, less urgent in tone, sees the spiritual life as a long progress with varying intensity of power. We have seen that in *The Cloud* we can recognize the prayers of acquired and infused recollection of later writers, and an adumbration, at least, of the night of sense. Hilton anticipates even more strikingly the Spanish mystics with his

[7] Dom Noetinger in the French edition (above, note 2) notes also references to the *Vitae Patrum*, John Cassian, St Bernard (especially *Sermons on the Canticle* and *De gradibus humilitatis*), Anselm (*Cur Deus Homo*) and St Thomas. Dr Benedict Hackett, O.E.S.A., in an article shortly to be published, demonstrates clearly that Hilton used William Flete's *De emendatione vitae*. This may have bearing on the dates of Hilton's work.

map of the route to Jerusalem, the vision of peace, and his
"night of murk" through which the soul has to pass.

The book in its present form as has been said, is divided
into two parts. In the first, Hilton enunciates for his ancress
the end of all her strivings, union with God in contemplation, and gives in outline the degrees of progress, but the
bulk of the first part is taken up with a description of the
means by which the soul may prepare the way to perfection
by destroying the image of sin within itself, and thus
achieving a resemblance to the image of God. The book
ends before the reforming of the soul has issued in the new
life of contemplation. On a later occasion the writer was
asked for further teaching concerning the two images, and
Hilton answered by continuing his account of the soul's
growth. But now the contemplative or mystical element,
which had fallen into the background, comes to the fore, and
Hilton clarifies the distinction between the active, ascetic life,
the "reformation in faith", and the contemplative, mystical
life, the "reformation in feeling". These two phrases may at
first cause trouble to one familiar with the terms of the six-
teenth-century Carmelite school of spirituality led by St
John of the Cross. There, a similar distinction is made between "faith" and "feeling", but in Carmelite language faith
is the theological virtue, the only adequate means by which
the soul may reach divine things with the mind, and "feeling" is the perception by senses or imagination, which must
be regarded as worthless in the progress towards God. With
Hilton, on the other hand, "faith" is used in the ordinary
sense as the holding of some truth which one can neither see
nor comprehend on the authority of God or the Church, and
"feeling" is what we should call mystical or supernatural
experience or perception. As Hilton puts it:

> This reform may be of two kinds: one in faith only, the other
> in faith and in feeling. . . . The first may be had easily, and in a

short time, the second only after a long time and with great spiritual labour. . . . The first kind of reform belongs only to beginners and those who are making progress in the spiritual life, and to men leading the active life. The second is for the perfect and for contemplative souls.[8]

The first reform in faith is, in fact, that accomplished by the soul in actively ridding itself of vices by the help of grace and with no perception of God other than the certainty of faith; it is the attempt of the soul using its enlightened reason and the ordinary assistance of grace to conform itself to what it believes, but sees not. The reformation in feeling is that accomplished within the soul when it has a new supernatural knowledge of God in Himself and is possessed by God who then works in and upon it, so to say, not through or by it.

In full agreement with *The Cloud* and all the great spiritual masters Hilton insists upon the need of recollection and self-knowledge:

There is one activity which is of great value and, as I think, a highway to contemplation. . . . It is for a man to enter into himself and come to the knowledge of his own soul and its powers, its beauty and its blemishes. . . . This is at first a difficult and painful spiritual labour for those who give themselves to it earnestly. For it is a striving in the soul against the root of all sins, great and small, and this root is nothing else than a false, misguided self-love. . . . By this labour a man must withdraw his mind from the love of all earthly creatures, from vain thoughts, and images of all sensible things, and from all self-love. Then since it cannot find rest in the love and sight of Jesus Christ, it must needs suffer pain.

We may compare the words of Julian of Norwich:

I saw full surely that it behoveth [needs to be] that we should be in longing and in penance unto the time that we be led so deep into God that we verily and truly know our own soul. . . .

[8] II v 153-4; (238).

We may never come to the full knowing of God till we know
first clearly our own soul.[9]

Noverim me, noverim Te. Hilton echoes *The Cloud*, also, in
his account of the difficulties in the way, and the need to do
all in the love of Christ:

> This is a hard work, for useless thoughts will press on you to
> draw your mind down to them . . . you will find something,
> not Jesus whom you seek, . . . but an obscure and heavy image
> of your own soul.[10]
> Whoever thinks to come to the working and the full use of
> contemplation and not by this way, that is to say not by stead-
> fast mind of the precious manhood and the passion of Jesus
> Christ nor by fulness of virtues, he cometh not by the door, and
> therefore as a thief he shall be cast out. . . . For Christ is door and
> He is porter . . . no man may come to the contemplation of the
> Godhead, but he be first reformed by fulness of meekness and
> charity to the likeness of Jesu in His manhood.[11]

Like *The Cloud*, he distinguishes between the fully supernatural prayer of contemplation on the one hand, and
visions, bodily or imaginary, and sense-perceptions of pleasure on the other, and he, also, has a side-glance at Rolle:

> Thou mayst understand that visions or revelations . . . in
> bodily appearing or in imagining . . . or else in any other feel-
> ing in bodily wits . . . as any sensible heat as it were fire glowing
> and warming the breast . . . are not very contemplation, nor are
> they but simple and secondary, though they be good, in regard
> of ghostly virtues, and of ghostly knowing and loving of God.[12]

And therefore

> Thou shalt not suffer thine heart wilfully to rest, nor for to
> delight wholly, in no bodily feeling . . . but thou shalt hold them

---

[9] I xlii 61–2; (96); Julian, Long version lvi p. 135.   [10] I lii 83; (126).
          [11] I xcii 137–80 (221).   [12] I x 14–15; (19).

in thine own sight as they were right nought or little in regard of ghostly desire and of steadfast thinking on Jesus Christ, nor cleave the thought of thy heart too mickle upon them. But thou shalt seek that thou mightest come to the ghostly feeling [experience] of God, and that in that thou mightest know the wisdom of God, the endless might of our Lord Jesu Christ, the great goodness of Him in Himself and in His creatures. For this is contemplation and that other is none.[13]

Hilton clearly felt the great importance of this teaching, for he returned to it later towards the middle of his second book:

Hearing of delectable song or feeling of comfortable heat in the body or seeing of light

(the reference to Rolle is unmistakable).

These are not ghostly feelings, for ghostly feelings are felt in the powers of the soul, principally in understanding and love and little in imagination . . . when they [sc. sensible perceptions] are best they are but outward tokens of the inward grace that is felt in the powers of the soul.[14]

and he instances the wind and the tongues of fire of Pentecost. His disciple, perhaps with Rolle and his reputation in mind, was still unsatisfied. Are not those who see these visions then contemplatives?

Then askest thou, whether these souls be reformed in feeling or not. It seemeth yes, in as much as they have such great ghostly feelings, that other men that stand only in faith feel not of. Unto this I may say . . . that these ghostly feelings . . . are not the feelings which a soul shall have and feel in the grace of contemplation. I say not but that they are true and graciously given of God. But these souls that feel such are not yet reformed in feeling, nor have they not yet the gift of perfection

[13] I xii–xiii 18–19; (25–6).   [14] II xxx 236–7; (364).

nor the ghostly burning love in Jesu, as they may come to. And nevertheless often it seemeth otherwise that such souls feel more of the love of God than other that have the gift of perfection . . . so far forth that it seemeth to another man that they were aye ravished in love. And though me thinketh that it is not so, well I wot that these manner feelings and fervours of devotion . . . are gracious gifts of God sent into chosen souls, for to draw them out of worldly love . . . nevertheless, that the fervour is so much in outward showing is not only for greatness of love that they have, but it is for littleness and weakness of their souls, that may not bear a little touching of God . . . and therefore the least touching of love and the least sparkle of ghostly light . . . is so great and comfortable . . . that the soul is overtaken with it; and also it is so new and so sudden . . . that the soul may not suffer for to bear it, but bursteth and showeth it out in weeping, sobbing, and other bodily stirring . . . afterward, when love hath boiled out all the uncleanness of the soul by such great fervours, then is the love clean and standeth still . . . yet hath the soul much more love than it had before, though it show less outward . . . in the self wise falleth it of other souls that are progressing and far forth in grace. They feel oft times gracious touchings of the Holy Ghost in their souls, both in understanding and sight of ghostly things, and in affection of love, but yet they be not reformed in feeling, nor yet they are not yet perfect . . . nor have they not yet the full gift of contemplation.[15]

Another reference shows how pervasive the example of Rolle had been:

All men that speak of the fire of love know not well what it is . . . it is neither bodily, nor is it not bodily felt. A soul may feel it in prayer . . . but he feeleth it by no bodily wit. For though it be so, that if it work in a soul the body may turn into a heat . . . nevertheless the fire of love is not bodily, for it is only in the ghostly desire of the soul.[16]

[15] II xxix 226-8; (351-5).   [16] I xxvi 38; (59).

For Hilton, the goal of all endeavour is the abiding spiritual silence of the contemplative:

> the third manner of prayer is only in the heart without speech, by great rest and quietness of the body and of the soul . . . and of such men and women that by long travail bodily and ghostly, or else by such sharp smitings of love as I have before said, come into a rest of spirit so . . . that they may ever continually pray in their heart.[17]

In the first book Hilton is concerned almost entirely with the preparatory ascetic life, and in the second book he gives, more clearly than any previous writer, an account of the beginning of the active night of sense:

> When a man perceive the love of this world false and failing . . . he may not at once feel the love of God, but he must abide a while in the night for he may not suddenly come from that one light to that other, that is, from the love of the world to the perfect love of God. This night is nought else but a forbearing and a withdrawing of the thought of the soul from earthly things, by great desire and yearning for to love and see and feel Jesu and ghostly things. This is the night: for right as the night is dark and a hiding of all bodily creatures and a resting from bodily deeds, right so a man that setteth him fully for to think on Jesu and for to desire only the love of Him, is busy for to hide his thought from vain beholding and his affection from fleshly liking of all bodily creatures. . . . But this is a good night and a light darkness, for it is a stopping out of the false love of this world, and it is a nighing to the true day.[18]

His description merges into that of the passive night:

> If it be painful to thee . . . abide grace . . . and know thou well . . . thy darkness is not restful because of . . . uncleanness of thyself . . . but it shall by process through feeling of grace be more easy . . . and that is when thy soul through grace is made

[17] I xxxii 44; (71).   [18] II xxiv 205; (321).

so free ... and so gathered into itself, that it desire not to think
of right nought. This is a rich nought ... for though the soul
think not of any earthly thing nevertheless it is full busy to
think on Him. What thing then maketh this darkness? Soothly
nought else but a gracious desire for to have the love of Jesus.
For that desire ... draweth out of the heart all worldly vanities.
... Unless the conscience be made clean through fire of burning desire to Jesu in this darkness, the which wasteth and burn-
eth all wicked stirrings of pride, [the soul cannot receive infused knowledge]. ... This is then a good darkness and a rich
nought ... the grace of our Lord Jesu sent into my heart hath
slain in me and brought to nought all love of the world and I
wist not how . . . Thus biddeth the prophet: he who hath
walked in darkness and hath no light, let him hope in the
Lord, and rest himself upon his God ... and then shall He with
beams of ghostly light fulfil all the powers of the soul.[19]

The similarity between this passage and the poem "On a dark
night" with its commentary by St John of the Cross will
have been apparent to all readers. Hilton adds:

I say not that thou mayest do thus of thyself, for I know well
that our Lord Jesu bringeth all this to end, whereso He will.
For He only through His grace stirreth a soul, and bringeth it
into this darkness first, and then into light ... For He doth all:
He formeth and reformeth. My child, if thou pass through fire,
dread not, for the flame shall not hurt thee. It shall cleanse thee
from all fleshly filth, and make thee able for to receive ghostly
fire of the love of God.[20]

As the soul advances a deeper form of recollection is necessary:

It needeth a soul that would have knowing of ghostly things,
for to have first knowledge of itself ... and that is when a soul
is so gathered into itself, and departed from all beholding of all
earthly things, and from the use of bodily wits, that it feeleth

[19] II xxiv 206–xxvii 221; (323–45).   [20] II xxviii 222–5; (346–50).

itself as it is in its own kind without a body. . . . Thy soul shall not rest still in this knowing, but it shall by this seek higher knowing above itself, and that is, the being of God.[21]

The chapter from which this last extract is taken and its neighbours are some of the weightiest and most penetrating in *The Scale*. Like the author of *The Cloud*, Hilton preaches the primacy of love, and while he rests upon a basis of Thomist thought, he rises to the teaching of the Rhineland school on the infused virtues:

> For [= since] love cometh out of knowing, and not knowing out of love, therefore it is said that in knowing and in sight principally of God with love is the bliss of a soul, and the more He is known the better He is loved . . . but love is the cause why a soul cometh to this sight and to this knowing . . . not the love that a soul hath in itself to God, but the love that our Lord hath to a sinful soul.[22]

And he goes on to define, even more accurately than *The Cloud*, the distinction between what theologians know as "operant" and "co-operant" grace:

> We do right nought but suffer Him [*sc.* the Holy Spirit] and assent to Him; for that is the most we do, that we assent wilfully to His gracious working in us. And yet is that will not of us, but of His making; so that me thinketh that He doth in us all that is well done, and yet we see it not. . . .[23]

And again, still more clearly:

> He is all, and He doth all . . . thou art nought else but a reasonable instrument wherein that he worketh[24] . . . then is the soul

---

[21] II xxx 229; (356–8).

[22] II xxxiv 247; (380–1). Cf. *Bonum Est* (*Minor Works*, ed. D. Jones, 1927, p. 186): "Where knowing faileth, there love hitteth. That I know not, I love best. . . . My love and my troth may touch thee and pass above all thy works even to thee, but my knowing is too little and may not go so far."

[23] II xxxiv 251–2; (385).   [24] II xxiv 203; (318).

more suffering than doing, and that is clear love. Thus St Paul
meant when he said: Whosoever are led by the Spirit of God,
they are the sons of God . . . who work not of themselves, but
suffer the Holy Ghost to stir them and work in them the feelings of love with a full sweet accord to his stirrings. . . . Other
souls cannot love thus, but travail themselves by their own
affections and stir themselves through thinking of God . . .
They do well and needfully, so be that they will know meekly
that their working is not kindly the gracious feeling [i.e. the
infused experience] of love, but it is a manly doing by a soul
at the bidding of reason.[25] The gift of prophecy, the gift of
miracle-working . . . are great gifts of the Holy Ghost, but
they are not the Holy Ghost, for a reproved soul might have all
those gifts [i.e. the *gratiae gratis datae*] . . . But the gift of love
is the Holy Ghost, God Himself . . . love unformed . . . the
bringeth love into the soul the fullhead of virtues . . . through
the gift of love that is the Holy Ghost.[26]

As the Holy Ghost is sent by Christ, His works are those of
Christ:

I Jesu . . . am God. . . . I do all your good deeds, and all your
good thoughts and all your good loves in you, and ye do right
nought. And yet nevertheless be these deeds called yours, not
because thou workest there principally, for I give them to you
for love that I have to you.[27] . . . For God worketh in us all,
both good will and good work.[28]

He is clear that contemplation is a development, in higher
degree and in fuller measure, of the sanctifying grace common to all baptized Christians who are not averted from
God by grave sin:

And this grace is not another grace than a chosen soul feeleth
in beginning of his conversion; but it is the same and the self
grace . . . for grace waxeth with the soul and the soul waxeth

[25] II xxxv 254; (389). [26] II xxxvi 256-8; (342-5).
[27] *Ibid.*, 257-8; (394). [28] II xxxv 255; (390).

with grace, and the more clean that a soul is . . . the more mighty is the grace, more inward and more ghostly showing the presence of our Lord Jesu.[29]

Infused love has also a purifying effect; by its touch the soul

is clean from all the filth of sin . . . all unordained affection of any creature is suddenly washed and wiped away, that there is no mean letting atwixt Jesu and the soul, but only the bodily life.[30]

Hilton nowhere explicitly poses the question that has so much exercised mystical theologians since the sixteenth century, whether the contemplative life is, under God, attainable by all. Implicitly, however, he equates it with perfection, blames those who make no attempt to progress in virtue and certainly suggests that "reform in feeling" is the end of a soul's endeavour. He realizes that few arrive thither and, like St John of the Cross, seeks to explain this. Many, when "reformed in faith" decide to go no further, which inevitably implies at least a relative deterioration, for "a soul may not stand still alway in one state".[31] Others, he thinks, become wedded to a certain round of religious exercises and will not change; they become petrified; they lack freedom of spirit. He can only repeat his conviction that

reforming in faith is the lowest state of all chosen souls, for beneath that might they not well be; but reforming in feeling is the highest state in this life that the soul may come to. . . . No man is made suddenly sovereign in grace, but through long exercise and silent working a soul may come thereto, namely when He helpeth and teacheth a wretched soul . . . for

[29] II xl 278; (423).
[30] II xl 273; (417). Cf. St John of the Cross, *Living Flame*, §29 (Peers, III, 134): "The webs which can hinder this union of the soul with God are three . . . the third is only the union of the soul in the body, which is sensual and animal life."
[31] II xviii 185; (291).

without special help and inwardly teaching of Him may no soul come thereto.[32]

The later chapters of the second book contain many descriptions of the effects of the grace of contemplation in the soul. Hilton, again like *The Cloud*, does not touch upon the highest point to which the soul made perfect may attain; there is nothing to set against the many chapters in *The Living Flame* and *The Spiritual Canticle* of St John of the Cross that describe the spiritual marriage and the life of the soul on ever higher levels. The reader can scarcely doubt that Hilton himself had experience of the earlier stages, at least, which in the scheme of later mystical theologians would be called the preparation of the soul for the spiritual betrothal. He also describes what in St John's terminology would be known as "formal words" and "substantial words" and "touches of union". Hilton is always sober in his language and without a trace of introspection or self-advertisement, but it is difficult not to see in the passages that follow an account of his own experience:

For God openeth the eyes of the soul and showeth to the soul the sight of Jesus wonderfully, and the knowing of Him, as the soul may suffer it thus by little and by little; and by that sight He raiseth all the affection of the soul to Him. . . . And then beginneth the soul to know Him ghostly . . . then seeth the soul somewhat of the kind [= nature] of the blessed Godhead of Jesu . . . this love is nought else but Jesu himself, that for love worketh all this in a man's soul and reformeth it in feeling to his likeness. This love may not be had by man's own travail, as some think. It is freely had of the gracious gift of Jesu.[33]

For know thou well that all the business that Jesu maketh about a soul is for to make it a true perfect spouse to Him in the fullness and highness of love. Because that may not be done suddenly, therefore Jesu, that is love and of all lovers wisest, assayeth by many wiles and by many wonderful means or it may come about.[34]

And then beginneth the soul to perceive a little of the privities of the blessed Trinity . . . then is it opened soothfastly to the eyes of the soul the onehead in substance and distinction of persons in the blessed Trinity, as it may be seen here . . . wonder great love feeleth the soul with heavenly delight in beholding of this soothfastness, when it is made through special grace; for love and light go both together in a clean soul.[35]

Hilton throughout *The Scale* so clearly presupposes a background and daily life of Catholic piety and practice that it is unnecessary to labour the point. It has been suggested, and may well be the case, that appearance of active "heresy" and criticism of traditional devotion in the neighbourhood of his home led him to retreat from the colder and more abstract phrases of *The Cloud* to an explicit and frequent mention of the humanity of Christ. Certainly many pages of Hilton are as evangelical in their piety as any of Wyclif's, and far more deeply tender in their expressions of the personal love of Jesus. But his doctrine is the same throughout, and is in full agreement with that of *The Cloud* on the one hand, and that of Julian of Norwich on the other.

No final judgment can be given on Hilton's prose style until a critical edition of his works has been published, but the reader of the modernized versions has the impression that it is less distinctive, if perhaps smoother, than either that of *The Cloud* or that of Julian. He is not, as they are in their different ways, the master of the arresting phrase and the short, lapidary sentence. An example of his style at its best is the well-known series of chapters, so excellently paraphrased in Father Baker's *Sancta Sophia*, comparing the spiritual life

[34] II xliv 301; (453).   [35] II xlvi 306–7; (461–2).

to a pilgrimage to Sion. Another passage may be quoted to show his peculiarly vivid way of commenting on a piece of Scripture:

"Make mirth with me and melody, for I have found my groat which I had lost." This groat is Jesus which thou hast lost, and if thou wilt find him, light up a lanthorn, that is God's Word, as David saith; "Thy Word is as a lanthorn to my feet." . . . If thou do so, thou shalt see all the dust, all the filth and small motes in thy house (for he is light itself)—that is to say, all fleshly loves and fears in thy soul. I mean not perfectly all; for as David saith; "Who knoweth all his trespasses?" As who should say, no man. Thou shalt cast out of thy heart all such sins, and sweep thy soul clear with the besom of the fear of God, and wash it with thy tears, and so shalt thou find thy groat, Jesus; he is thy groat, thy penny, thy heritage. This groat will not be found so easily as it is thought, for this work is not of one hour, nor of one day, but many days and years, with much sweat and swink of body and travail of soul. If thou cease not, but seek busily, sigh and sorrow deeply, mourn stilly, and stoop low, till thine eyes water for anguish and for pain, for that thou hast lost thy treasure Jesus, at the last (when his will is) well shalt thou find thy groat Jesus. When thou hast found him, as I have said—that is, when in purity of conscience thou feelest the familiar and peaceful presence of that blessed man Jesus Christ, at least a shadow or a glimmering of him— thou mayest, if thou wilt, call all thy friends to thee, to make mirth with thee, for that thou hast found thy groat Jesus.[36]

In spite of the original destination of the first part of *The Scale* for an ancress, and of the deep mystical appeal of the whole work, Hilton's book became, more than any other spiritual writing, a well-known and widely read manual, and his teaching helped to form many of the most religious souls in the restless and materialistic century that followed his death. Owing, no doubt, to his sane and methodical presentation of

[36] I xlviii 76–8; (116–18).

the ascetic life, he was a devotional classic when printing was first introduced into England, and as such was printed by Wynkyn de Worde in 1494. It is from the dedication to this edition that we learn that *The Scale* was often in the hands of that masterful but gentle lady, the Lady Margaret, mother of Henry Tudor and friend and penitent of Bishop Fisher, *felix opportunitate mortis*, whose benefactions to learning have made her name and character known to many generations of those who have lived upon her foundations.

Chapter VII

JULIAN OF NORWICH

WITH Julian of Norwich we approach a mystic of quite another appearance.[1] Both the author of *The Cloud* and Walter Hilton were primarily teachers and directors, instructing their disciples in the elements of the contemplative life, and though each gives implicit evidence of having known at first hand something, at least, of the mystical way to which they are directing others, neither bases any instruction or illustration specifically on his personal experience. Julian, on the other hand, owes all that she has to say at least ostensibly to her own reception of spiritual communications. She begins her book with an account of her "shewings", dated in time and place, and all that follows is a penetration of their meaning.

Julian, whose baptismal name and surname are unknown, tells us herself that she was thirty and a half years old in May, 1373, and we know from Norwich wills that she was, at

---

[1] Though Julian of Norwich has probably found more readers and a wider popularity in the present century than either *The Cloud* or Hilton, she has been slow in attracting the attention of scholars, and her *Revelations* are still (1960) available only in quasi-popular editions, with no critical text. This lack will soon, it is hoped, be supplied by a volume in the Early English Text series, to be edited by Fr James Walsh, S.J., and Sister Anna Maria Reynolds, C.P., and the latter has already published a text (without apparatus) with a valuable introduction and brief notes (see below, note 2). Meanwhile an extremely able and thorough examination has been made of Julian's credentials and doctrine by Fr P. Molinari, S.J. (*Julian of Norwich: the teaching of a Fourteenth Century English Mystic*, London, 1958), while scattered references have been assembled in various studies, and Miss H. E. Allen in her notes on *The Book of Margery Kempe* (below, p. 142) has indicated some of the contemporary influences that may have affected her.

least in later years, a recluse at St Julian's church at Carrow, within the bounds of the city, and that she was alive in 1416, when she would have been by any standards a very old woman. She received a number of small legacies, and we know from the book of Margery Kempe, who visited her probably between 1400 and 1410, that she had a considerable reputation as counsellor in spiritual matters. She may have been previously a nun at the Benedictine priory of Carrow, the owner of the church, but there is no evidence for this, whereas there is considerable probability that she was still living at home when the "shewings" of 1373 took place. These shewings, which determined the course of her spiritual life, have come down to us in two forms, known as the Long and the Shorter Versions.² As both are unquestionably authentic, although the manuscript of the shorter version is the oldest, the natural supposition would be that the shorter was an abbreviation of the longer. Nevertheless, competent editors are agreed that the shorter, of which the manuscript is the earliest extant, is the earlier, and that the longer issues from the reflections and enlightenment which Julian received during the twenty or thirty years that elapsed between the writing of the two books.³

Julian refers to herself as "unlettered", and scholars have been curiously ambivalent in their treatment of her literacy. The question is probably less important than it may seem. St

² Julian, like the other English mystics, was re-discovered by the English Benedictines of the seventeenth century. Dom Serenus Cressy printed in 1670 the *Long Text* from what is now Paris B.N. Fonds anglais 40; this was reprinted by G. H. Parker (Leicester, 1843) and Fr Tyrrell (London, 1902). Meanwhile Fr P. H. Collins had printed the same text from B. M. Sloane 2499; he was followed by Miss G. Warrack in 1901 and Dom G. R. Hudleston in 1927. The *Short Text* was first printed by Rev. D. Harford from Brit. Mus. Addit. MS 37,790 in 1911 (often reprinted); Sister A. M. Reynolds printed from this in 1958. References in this chapter will be to the editions of Warrack, *Long Text*, (W) and Reynolds, *Short Text*, (R) by chapter and page.

³ This is the judgment of both Harford and Reynolds, and would seem certain.

Catherine of Siena could not write and it is generally accepted that Margery Kempe dictated her memoirs. In Margery's case the scribe probably polished the narrative, but St Catherine's letters are commonly regarded as her *ipsissima verba*. Whether dictated or not, the same is certainly true of Julian, and her title as "the first English woman of letters" is not necessarily nonsense. We who live in an age of dictated books cannot deny the title of author to one who never puts pen to paper. We can at least feel fairly confident that her scribe, if there was one, was no more than an amanuensis.

We know nothing of Julian or her life before the shewings occurred, but it is clear that she had long been an exceptionally devout woman; such slight evidence as exists suggests that she was still living at home with her mother, for whom she had a deep affection. She herself tells us that at some unspecified time previously she had desired three favours of God. The first was a "bodily sight" of the Passion of Christ in order that she might share in His sufferings by love as did His Mother. The second was to have "of God's giving, a bodily sickness" in order that, by suffering all the pains, physical, mental and spiritual, of imminent death she might be purified in mind and heart from all love of earthly things. The third was for three "wounds": of sorrow for sin; of suffering with Christ; and of longing for God. She asked the first two favours with the condition "if God so will", for she felt them to be outside normal experience, but she asked for the third absolutely. She tells us also that the desire for the two former graces passed from her mind, and this, even with our knowledge of the subconscious self, must at least mean that she did not consciously continue her prayer or wish for them.[4]

The illness, however, duly befell her when she was "thirty years old and a half" on 3–8 May, 1373. She describes some

[4] W ii 3–5; R i 1–3.

of her symptoms very vividly, but it is useless to enquire what the illness was, or indeed whether it was organic or infective or, in part at least, hysteric. Those who feel that Julian was an exceptionally honest and clearsighted woman, and who read the carefully described details, will not readily dismiss the whole incident as hysteria. While it is true that some of the best recorded lives of the saints include serious and inexplicable illnesses in early life which may be the result of an intensive inner conflict of which the patient was hardly aware, we may remember that there are still purely patho-logical conditions which baffle diagnosis. Julian certainly suffered the pains of the dying and was thought by all around her, including her mother and parish priest, to be on the point of death:

> On the fourth night, I took all my rites of Holy Church, and weened not to have liven till day. And after this I lingered on two days and two nights, and on the third night I weened often-times to have passed, and so weened they that were with me. ... And they that were with me sent for the parson my curate to be at mine ending. He came, and a child with him, and brought a cross.[5]

When all strength, breath and eyesight were failing, and the priest held up the crucifix before her face, she suddenly felt all pain to cease, and it occurred to her to desire the wound of compassion for our Lord's sufferings. She expressly tells us that she desired no "bodily sight", but suddenly the crucifix before her eyes changed:

> And in this suddenly I saw the red blood trickling down from under the garland of thorns hot and fresh and right plenteously ... like to the drops of water that fall off the eaves of a house after a great shower of rain ... and for the roundness, they were like to the scale of herring.[6]

[5] W iii 5; R ii 4–5.   [6] W iv 8, vii 16; R ii 7.

Henceforward, the shewings succeeded one another; so far as we can gather, the sight of our Lord's head on the crucifix was present to her all the time, though undergoing changes, while to her mind and soul came "words" and "ghostly shewings". These took a considerable time:

> The first began early in the morning about the hour of four: and it lasted shewing by process full fair and steadily, each following other till it was nine of the day overpassed.[7]

The last shewing took place in the following night, and when it ended her feeling of illness returned. The return of pain weakened her mind, and for a moment she lost faith in the reality of what she had seen:

> Then came a religious person to me, and asked me how I fared. I said I had raved that day.[8]

She fell asleep, and while asleep saw, or dreamed, that she was assaulted by the devil. It is noticeable that she distinguishes this from the manner of the other visions:

> And in the sleep, at the beginning, *methought* the Fiend set him on my throat . . . This ugly shewing was made sleeping, and so was none other.

She waked and

> Anon a light smoke came in the door, with a great heat and a foul stench. I said, "Benedicite Dominus, it is all on fire that is here!" And I weened it had been a bodily fire. I asked them that were with me if they felt any stench; they said nay they felt none; I said, "Blessed be God," for that I wist well it was the fiend that was come.[9]

Whatever we may think of this, Julian's accuracy is very noteworthy. She saw this as a different way from the "shewings". Though invisible to others, it appeared to her as

[7] W lxv 164.   [8] W lxvi 165.   [9] *Ibid.*, 165–6.

visible smoke and perceptible stench and heat, whereas the shewings impressed themselves upon her mind at once as spiritual.

Immediately after this visitation she made an act of faith in the revelations which had been made to her, and which she had for a time doubted. On the same evening she had a final shewing, and it was followed by more diabolical assaults, which lasted for most of the night and till about prime in the morning.

This brief summary can convey no impression of the extreme vividness and simplicity of Julian's narrative; it is an artless masterpiece. There have been, before and since, visionaries who have described the Passion or some of its incidents. Julian differs from almost all of them in two respects at least: the pictorial element is small, and though vivid, indeed extremely so, is in a sense abstract rather than photographic, and, secondly, this element is altogether subordinate. The "bodily sight" does little more than release a deeper shewing in the understanding, and this in turn leads, not at once, but over a space of many years, to a purely spiritual and largely incommunicable sight or contemplation of the divine truth behind the two previous forms of manifestation. As she herself says:

> All the blessed teaching of our Lord God was shewed to me in these parts, as I have said before. That is to say: by the bodily sight, and by words formed in my understanding, and by ghostly sight. For the bodily sight, I have said what I saw, as truly as I can. And for the words formed, I have said them right as our Lord shewed me them. And for the ghostly sight, I have said somewhat, but I may never fully tell it.[10]

As far as we can gather from her writings, Julian had no further "shewing". We are told, however, that her question-

[10] R xxiii 73.

ing as to the meaning of one of the shewings was answered
fifteen years later "in ghostly understanding" and one of the
shewings, the fourteenth and hardest, was made clear to her
twenty years less three months from the original occurrence.[11] These two passing references show that the happenings of the eighth of May were for her an abiding and un-
replaced source of meditation.

The divisions into which Julian herself arranges her shewings—"bodily sight", "ghostly in bodily likeness", "more
ghostly without bodily likeness" and "ghostly sight"—have
been taken by some to represent the three divisions of
visionary experiences, originally formulated by St Augustine
and reproduced by all medieval mystical theologians including St Thomas, and thenceforward considered as
classical. These are the "corporeal", i.e. accepted as sense-
perceptions; the "imaginary", i.e. perceptions by the internal senses; and the "intellectual", i.e. pure knowledge
received either by way of infused ideas or substantial words
or in some still higher spiritual way. An able theologian has,
however, recently argued with great show of probability that
none of Julian's shewings was in the strict sense corporeal, for
she retained her critical power of questioning its physical
normality. He would therefore catalogue Julian's "bodily
shewing" and others which she describes as "ghostly in bodily
likeness" as imaginative visions, whereas those of "ghostly
sight" or "more ghostly without bodily likeness" would fall
into the two divisions, current among theologians, of lower
or higher intellectual visions.[12]

However that may be, Julian herself clearly regarded the
teaching contained in the revelations as God-given:

But God forbid that ye should say . . . that I am a teacher, for
I do not mean that . . . For I am a woman, unlettered, feeble,

[11] W lxxxvi 202 "fifteen years", i.e. 1388; li 110 "twenty years" i.e. 1393.
[12] Molinari, *op. cit.*

and frail. But I know well this that I say, I have it on the shewing of him who is sovereign truth, and truly charity urgeth me
to tell you of it ... to the more hating of sin and loving of God.[13]

At the same time it was in perfect accordance with the
teaching of the Church:

for all things in this blessed shewing of our Lord I beheld as
one with the teaching of Holy Church ... and never did I
understand a thing therein which harms me or withdraws me
from the true teaching of Holy Church.[14]

She is likewise emphatic that the shewings of themselves are
no proof of holiness in the recipient, and that faith and love
alone benefit the soul:

Because of the shewing I am not good, but only if I love God
the better. . . . I am certain there are full many who never had
shewing nor sight but of the common teaching of Holy Church,
and who love God better than I. For a soul that only fasteneth
itself on to God with very trust ... it is most worship that it
may do to him, as to my sight.[15]

Julian herself, therefore, is in full agreement with the common teaching of mystical theologians that visions of themselves are not mystical graces, i.e. graces that are an essential
part of the mystical or contemplative life. It is another question whether some of the later "ghostly" shewings may not
have been some of those "lofty manifestations of knowledge"
which according to St John of the Cross "can only come to
the soul that attains to union with God",[16] and whether many
of the expressions used in the later and fuller version of the
revelations do not make it clear that by then, at least, Julia
was a contemplative.

Julian's editors have thought to find an order in the shewings, but while the individual topics are clear enough it would

[13] R vi 17. [14] R vi 17–18. [15] R vi 15–16.
[16] *Ascent of Mount Carmel*, II, xxvi (Peers, I, 196).

seem difficult to find an overall sequence of thought. It is impossible here to do more than glance at two or three of the leading topics, but the depth of her thought can only be grasped by a careful reading of the whole. We may take as a sample her teaching on the Blessed Virgin. It begins with her sight of the young Mother:

> In this Shewing he brought our Blessed Lady to my understanding. I saw her ghostly, in bodily likeness: a simple maid and a meek, young of age and little waxen above a child, in the stature that she was when she conceived. Also God shewed me in part the wisdom and truth of her soul, knowing the greatness of her Maker and the littleness of herself that was made . . . In this sight I understood soothly that she is more than all that God made beneath her in worthiness and grace; for above her is nothing that is made but the blessed Manhood of Christ.[17]

Later she saw the Mother by the Cross:

> Here I saw a part of the compassion of our lady Saint Mary: for Christ and she were so oned in love that the greatness of her loving was cause of the greatness of her pain . . . for ever the mightier, the sweeter, that the love be, the more sorrow it is to the lover to see that body in pain that is loved.[18]

A little after this:

> Our Lord said . . . "Wilt thou see her?" And in this sweet word it was as if he said . . . "Wilt thou see how I love her, that thou mightest joy with me the love that I have in her and she in me? . . . Wilt thou see in her how thou art loved? For thy love I made her so high, so noble, and so worthy" . . . And Jesus in this word shewed me ghostly sight of her . . . high and noble and glorious, and pleasing to him above all creatures. And he willeth that it be known; that so all those that please them in him should please them in her, and in the pleasance that he hath in her and she in him. And to more understand-

<hr>

[17] W iv 9; R iv 10.   [18] W xviii 40; R x 30.

ing, he shewed this example: As if a man love a creature
singularly, above all creatures, he willeth to make all creatures
to love and to have pleasance in that creature he loveth so
greatly.[19]

And Julian saw that Mary is Mother of all:

> For Christ having knit in him each man that shall be saved,
> is perfect man. Thus our Lady is our Mother in whom we are
> all enclosed and of her born in Christ: for she that is Mother
> of our Saviour is Mother of all that shall be saved in our
> Saviour; and our Saviour is our own very Mother, in whom
> we are endlessly borne.[20]

The last clause introduces us to a very characteristic piece
of Julian's teaching, the Motherhood of God. This devotion
was made familiar in western speculation by St Anselm, with
whose teaching Julian may have been acquainted,[21] but it is
clear that the concept of motherhood touched a very deep
chord in her own being. We may remember that her own
mother was by her during her grave illness, and made ready
to close her eyes when she supposed that her daughter was
dead. It is possible, also, that it was she in whose well-being
Julian took particular interest.[22] In any case, many of the
phrases that follow seem to reflect deep memories of acts of
love received in the past:

> Our Kind Mother, our Gracious Mother [sc. Jesus] for that
> he would all wholly become our Mother in all things, he took
> the ground of his works full low and full mildly in the Maiden's
> womb. . . . The Mother's service is nearest, readiest and surest:
> for it is most of truth. . . . We wit that all our mother's bearing

---

[19] W xxv 53; R xiii 37–8.   [20] W lvii 139–40.

[21] Cf. Dom André Cabassut, "Une dévotion médiévale peu connue: la
dévotion à Jésus 'notre mère'", in Révue d'ascétique et de Mystique, XCIX–C
(1949), April–December; also Sister A. M. Reynolds, "Some Literary Influences
in the Revelations of Julian of Norwich", in Leeds Studies in English and Kindred
Languages, nos. 7 and 8 (1952), 18 ff.

[22] W xxxv 60.

is the bearing of us to pain and to dying: and what is this but that our Very Mother, Jesus, he—All-Love—beareth us to joy and endless living? . . . The mother may give her child suck of her milk, but our precious Mother, Jesus, he may feed us with himself, and doeth it, full courteously and full tenderly, with the Blessed Sacrament that is precious food of very life. . . . This fair lovely word *Mother*, it is so sweet and kind itself that it may not verily be said of none but of him; and to her that is very Mother of him and of all.[23]

Only those who read the whole book will be able to realize how profoundly and yet how simply Julian gazes at the mysteries of the faith—at the Holy Trinity, the union of the Word with human nature, original sin and the Redemption. We may, indeed, wonder at the deep things that filled the mind of this secluded woman, and at the strength of intellect which strives to explain them. We must often feel that she has seen with her soul man and his destiny in the timeless aspect of the divine knowledge, and cannot fully reconcile this with what happens to him in the time-process.[24] Throughout she is clear that when she speaks in the first person she is speaking nevertheless of all Christian men: Christ's love, Christ's death, are all for her, but they are also all for each soul that shall be saved. She cannot see the individual, only all-man.

All readers will have been impressed by the optimism of Julian, though she is perfectly aware of weakness, suffering and sin, and though she holds firmly to the teaching of the Church on eternal damnation. The words with which she ends her book are familiar:

Wouldst thou wit thy Lord's meaning in this thing? Wit it well: Love was his meaning. Who shewed it thee? Love. What shewed he thee? Love. Wherefore shewed it he? For Love.[25]

[23] W lx 149–51. Cf. R 84–6.
[24] Cf. a valuable study by E. I. Watkin in *The English Way* (1933), 128–58.
[25] W lxxxvi 202.

There are many other passages of like meaning:

> And this word "Thou shalt not be overcome," was said full clearly and full mightily, for assuredness and comfort against all tribulations that may come. He said not: "Thou shalt not be tempested, thou shalt not be travailed, thou shalt not be dis-eased"; but he said: "Thou shalt not be overcome." God willeth that we take heed to these words, and that we be ever mighty in sure trust, in weal and woe. For he loveth and liketh us, and so willeth he that we love and like him and mightily trust in him; and all shall be well.[26]

> My dear darling, I am glad thou art come to me in all thy woe; I have ever been with thee, and now seest thou me loving, and we be oned in bliss.[27]

> Then said our good Lord Jesus Christ, "Art thou well apaid that I suffered for thee," I said, "Yea, good Lord, gramercy; yea, good Lord, blessed mote thou be." Then said Jesu our kind Lord, "If thou art apaid, I am apaid: it is a joy, a bliss, an endless liking to me, that ever I suffered passion for thee: and if I might suffer more, I would suffer more."[28]

Julian's shewings, however, are far from being simply assertions of the divine love. They treat of many of the deepest topics of nature and grace, of good and evil, of the hypostatic union of the divine and human natures in Christ, and of the identification with Christ, the inclusion in Christ, of all those predestined to eternal salvation. Nor is Julian ever self-centred, even when she is most individual; as she repeats emphatically:

> All that I say of me, I mean in person of all mine even Christian.[29]

That is to say, the love, the confidence given her from Christ is given to all the redeemed. Perhaps no passage of the shewings is more revealing than that where she is confronted by the problem of evil.

[26] W lxviii 170.   [27] W xl 82 (quotation above is from Collins's text).
[28] W xxii 46–7; R xii 34.   [29] W viii 19; R vi 15.

And so I beheld, generally, in all of us, and methought: "If sin had not been, we should all have been clean and like to our Lord, as he made us." And thus in my folly, afore this time often I wondered why by the great foreseeing wisdom of God the beginning of sin was not letted: for then, methought, all should have been well ... But Jesus answered ... "It behoved that there should be sin; but all shall be well, and all shall be well, and all manner of thing shall be well." In this naked word sin, our Lord brought to my mind, generally, all that is not good ... but I saw not sin: for I believe it hath no manner of substance nor no part of being, nor could it be known but by the pain it is cause of ... And for the tender love that our good Lord hath to all that shall be saved, he comforteth readily and sweetly, signifying thus: "It is sooth that sin is cause of all this pain; but all shall be well, and all shall be well, and all manner of thing shall be well." ... And in these words I saw a marvellous high mystery hid in God, which mystery he shall openly make known to us in heaven: in which knowing we shall verily see the cause why he suffered sin to come.[30]

Julian was, however, not yet fully satisfied, and in her thoughts she put the question, with all reverence:

"Ah! good Lord, how might all be well, for the great hurt that is come, by sin, to the creature?" ... And to this our blessed Lord answered full meekly and with lovely cheer, and shewed that Adam's sin was the most harm that ever was done, or ever shall be, to the world's end. ... Furthermore he taught that I should behold the glorious satisfaction; for this Amends-making is more pleasing to God and more worshipful, without comparison, than ever was the sin of Adam harmful. Then signifieth our blessed Lord thus in his teaching ... "For since I have made well the most harm, then it is my will that thou know thereby that I shall make well all that is less." He gave me to understand of two parts of truth. The one part is our Saviour and our salvation. This blessed part is open and clear

[30] W xxvii 55-7.

and fair and light, and plenteous. . . . In this willeth our Lord that we be occupied, joying in him . . . The other part is hid and shut up from us: that is to say, all that is beside our salvation. For it is our Lord's privy counsel, and it belongeth to the royal lordship of God to have his privy counsel in peace, and it belongeth to his servant, for obedience and reverence, not to learn wholly his counsel. And thus our good Lord answered to all the questions and doubts that I might make, saying full comfortably: "I may make all things well, I can make all things well, I will make all things well, and I shall make all things well; and thou shalt see thyself that all manner of thing shall be well."[31]

Even then Julian was not satisfied:

One point of our faith is that many creatures shall be condemned: as angels that fell out of heaven for pride . . . and . . . methought it was impossible that all manner of things should be well. . . . And as to this I had no other answer in shewing of our Lord God but this: "That which is impossible to thee is not impossible to me: I shall save my word in all things, and I shall make all things well."[32]

Finally:

And yet in this I desired, as far as I durst, that I might have full sight of Hell and Purgatory. . . . But for all my desire, I could see of this right nought. . . . For I saw soothly in our Lord's teaching, the more we busy us to know his secret counsel in this or any other thing, the farther shall we be from the knowing thereof.[33]

Julian does not set out, as do the author of *The Cloud* and Hilton, to give detailed instructions on prayer, but she has three chapters in which we can learn something of her mind. A careful theologian has recently analysed all her utterances, and has concluded that her doctrine is in all points in agree-

[31] W xxix–xxxi 60–2.   [32] W xxxii 66.   [33] W xxxiii 67.

ment with the teaching of St John of the Cross and classical mystical theology. We may accept this in gross, without feeling the need to find in her all the details of later writers.[34] We may also accept some very practical instructions that she gives:

> Therefore He saith thus: "Pray inwardly, though thee thinketh it savour thee not: for it is profitable, though thou feel not, though thou see nought; yea, though thou think thou canst not. For in dryness and in barrenness, in sickness and in feebleness, then is thy prayer well-pleasant to me, though thee thinketh it savour nought but little." . . . God accepteth the goodwill and travail of His servant, howsoever we feel.[35]

> Prayer oneth the soul to God . . . when our courteous Lord of his grace sheweth Himself to our soul, we have that we desire. And then we see not, for the time, what we should more pray, but all our intent with all our might is set wholly to be beholding of Him. And this is an high unperceivable prayer, as to my sight: for all the cause wherefore we pray, it is oned into the sight and beholding of Him to whom we pray; marvellously enjoying with reverent dread, and with so great sweetness and delight in Him, that we can pray right nought but as He stirreth us, for the time.[36]

In the foregoing pages we have constantly referred to the "shewings" and cited the "words" which Julian relates that she has seen and heard. Do we intend by so doing to accept her statements in their most literal sense and treat her experiences and her words as a direct communication from God?

---

[34] Fr Molinari, *op. cit.*, attempts at length to present a concordance between Julian and St John of the Cross, and Sister Reynolds, pp. lii–liii, gives parallels from St Teresa, but in fact Julian never treats (as do the author of *The Cloud* and Hilton) of the nature of mystical contemplation and the operation of grace (i.e. mystical theology as such); she records what she saw in her mind and soul and comments on this. So far as can be seen from her own words, she was not a contemplative in the sense defined above (p. 3) at the time of the shewings, though she would appear to have been raised habitually to infused prayer later.

[35] W xli 85–6.

[36] W xliii 90–1. This is unquestionably mystical, contemplative prayer.

Before replying we may reassert two essential principles. The first is, that as Christians we believe, not only that God can and does guide our lives by His individual providence, but that He can directly and immediately illuminate our minds and turn our hearts to Himself. It is therefore an essential difference between the Christian and other interpretations of the mystical experience that whereas others regard it as the direct result of some kind of activity or potentiality of the human spirit, we would maintain that it is, when authentic, the action of God Himself upon the faculties to which He has given power to receive that action in a manner denied to normal human nature. All genuine mysticism is therefore the direct action of God bestowing knowledge and love of Himself. As to the authenticity of any individual experience, we can do no more than judge the sanity and good faith of the claimant, and the intrinsic worth and good effect of the experience itself.

The second principle is that already enunciated on an earlier page: that while the human spirit is in this life it is unable to comprehend God as He is, still less to feel or to see Him. In the mystical life, and what may be called the direct preparation for the mystical life, the only purpose of God is to sanctify and illuminate the soul. God gives as God, but the divine influence is received according to the disposition of the recipient, and it may then be translated into terms of sight and word by the faculties which are not strong enough to receive the illumination in a direct, supernatural, incommunicable manner. These sights and words may be to a greater or lesser degree a faithful translation of the inpouring of God's grace, but they are not directly and of themselves God-given. They are the creature's translation of a divine influence, and as such inevitably degrade and distort the message to a greater or less degree.

In Julian's case her transparent sincerity and the theological accuracy of her words are strong arguments for the authenticity of the incommunicable experience. The distortion may be small, and she may succeed in giving in words the nearest approximation to the supernatural truth, but there are several passages in her book where she fails, and clearly realizes her failure, to translate into words what her soul has seen. She has seen the truth in the supreme wisdom which can embrace seeming contradictions, but when she comes to use human thought and language, the unity is broken and the apparent contradictions remain.

Julian of Norwich is, in qualities of mind and heart, one of the most remarkable—perhaps the most remarkable—Englishwoman of her age. Her mind can wrestle with the deepest mysteries of theology and life, and has absorbed (or discovered for itself) much of the abstruse technical phraseology of the schools. At the same time she shows herself a generous and loving woman with an extraordinary delicacy of feeling, and she is able to express this in language which goes directly home to the heart, and yet is in no way rough or oversimple, for she has also a vivid pictorial memory and a wide range of words. In her sobriety, as in her depth, she deserves to rank very high among the women mystics of the middle ages.

The English mystics, and in particular the three who lived and wrote between 1350 and 1400, are indeed a remarkable group. Those who know only the political and material history of the fourteenth century in England are justified in thinking it an age of confusion, of disunion and of disaster, with no great men of action or statecraft or wisdom to redeem the times. The last decade of the reign of Edward III and the whole of the reign of Richard II are full of intrigue and violence and political unwisdom, and neither the Church in its official representatives, nor the brilliant colours of the decaying chivalry can clothe with real nobility the apparent barrenness of mental and spiritual life. Yet in the last years of Edward III Hilton and Julian, Langland and St John of Bridlington, the author of *The Cloud* and Thomas de la Mare were all at the height of their powers, nearer to us in their dealings with their fellows and in their vision of things eternal than any equal number of their fellow-countrymen in the next century. Christopher Dawson, writing almost thirty years ago, remarked of Langland that he was the first and last great poet to be entirely Catholic and English in his outlook, the authentic voice of this country after seven centuries of Christian faith and untouched by any foreign influence. The same might be said of all our English mystics. They may have received, directly or indirectly, some of the more speculative elements of their teaching from abroad, though what they received was rather the Christian tradition than anything coloured by a foreign cast of thought, but in their practical instruction and in their self-revelation there is nothing that is not purely and racily English.

It is not surprising, therefore, that their writings were prized and read by their countrymen and countrywomen so long as the old religion endured. No others rose to continue their tradition or to supplant them. When the conservative *élite* went into exile and the religious life was reborn in France and the Low Countries manuscripts of the English mystics went with them, and copies of Rolle and Hilton's printed works, and when, in the early years of the seventeenth century, Father Augustine Baker treated of the contemplative life with his fellow-monks and nuns, he made *The Cloud* their manual and wrote a commentary upon it. A few decades later, Serenus Cressy, the distinguished Oxford convert who was an ardent disciple of Baker and the editor of his remains, himself published the first printed edition of Julian. From that time till the epoch of the Catholic Revival and the Oxford Movement the English mystics faded out of the consciousness of English Catholics. Then, in the late 'sixties and early 'seventies of the nineteenth century Hilton, *The Cloud* and Julian were all reprinted. Then again silence fell till the general interest in mystical writings of all sorts revived in the first decade of the present century. Since then editions of all the mystics, critical and popular, have multi-plied, and linguistic scholars have joined their labours to those of devotional editors.

Chapter VIII

MARGERY KEMPE

W HEN the predecessor of the present book appeared, thirty years and more ago, Margery Kempe was known only as the author of a series of extracts printed as a "short treatise" by Wynkyn de Worde of Fleet Street, London, in 1501, and extant only in a single copy in the Cambridge University Library, from which the passages were reprinted by Henry Pepwell in 1521,[1] and again, in modern English, by Edmund Gardner in 1910. De Worde entitled his pamphlet *A shorte treatyse of contemplacyon taught by our lorde Jhesu cryste, or taken out of the boke of Margerie kempe of Lynn.* Pepwell in his reprint (followed by Gardner) added the word *ancresse* after the name of the authoress, and this, and the general style of the extracts, led modern critics not unnaturally to assume that they had to do with another mystic of the type of Julian of Norwich. As we now know, these passages were all carefully chosen devotional extracts, containing no narrative or personal matter, and, apart from their purport as conversations between Margery and Christ or the Blessed Virgin, they have nothing extraordinary about them. De Worde had modernized and standardized the language and had made numerous verbal changes.

So matters rested till 1934, when one of those unexpected

[1] W. de Worde's treatise has been reprinted in *The Book of Margery Kempe* (Early English Text Society original series 212, 1940), Appendix II, pp. 353–7, with collation of Pepwell's text and references to the relevant passages from M. Kempe's *Book*. It is discussed *ibid.*, xlvi–xlvii.

discoveries was made that encourage scholars and historians never to despair. Colonel W. Butler-Bowdon, the representative of an old Yorkshire Catholic family, sent up to the Victoria and Albert Museum for examination a neglected manuscript that had been "in the possession of [his] family from time immemorial", and this was identified by Miss Hope Emily Allen as the lost *Book* of Margery Kempe. Notes and other indications in the manuscript, which was probably written at Lynn *c.* 1440–50, showed that it had been in the possession of the Yorkshire Charterhouse of Mount Grace shortly before the Dissolution. A modernized version, with the title *Margery Kempe*, was published by Col. Butler-Bowdon in 1936, and a full critical edition, edited by Professor S. B. Meech, with copious introductions and annotations by himself and Miss Allen, was published by the Early English Text Society in 1940. Miss Allen therein promised a further instalment of notes on Margery's predecessors, for which scholars have hitherto waited eagerly, but in vain.

The *Book of Margery Kempe*, thus made available and interpreted for all to read, was recognized at once as a godsend and as a disillusionment. On the one hand it proved to be, not merely a devotional work but a full-scale autobiography (the earliest in the language) of a remarkable woman, providing new and invaluable information on contemporary religious and social conditions; on the other hand, the book is not in any real sense a treatise on contemplation, and Margery herself, however interesting a figure she may be to the student of religious sentiment or psychology, is clearly not the equal of the earlier English mystics in depth of perception or wisdom of spiritual doctrine, nor as a personality can she challenge comparison with Julian of Norwich.

Margery Kempe, whose family relationships and connections in Lynn were quickly established from the unusually

abundant medieval records of the town,[2] which is the first
corporation known to have used English for its civic documents, was born c. 1373 at Bishop's (later King's) Lynn in
Norfolk, the daughter of a prosperous burgess John Brun-
ham, who was mayor of the town in 1370 and repeatedly in
after years. She married c. 1393 John Kempe, who also was a
well-to-do townsman and official of Lynn, and by him she
had, in course of time, fourteen children, of whom only a son
(who himself died long before his mother) is mentioned in
the *Book*. After the birth of her first child she was out of her
wits for eight months, and recovered, according to her own
account, after a vision of Christ, and thenceforward regarded
herself as bound to a life of particular devotion, with fasts
and penances, though for some years she retained many of the
faults, vanities and even the sins, of a worldly woman.
Then, so we gather, she was gradually weaned to a life of
prayer and more solid penance. She tells us little about the
fifteen years that followed her first unusual experience, save
that she continued to bear children and run her home, not
without various misfortunes, but in 1413 she persuaded her
husband to live with her in perfect chastity, and thenceforward the narrative of her life is consecutive and fairly full
till 1418, and then again, after a gap, from 1433 to 1434. These
two long runs of narrative cover her pilgrimages to the Holy
Land and Italy, 1413–15, to Compostella, 1417–18, and a
journey to Danzig and a return by land through Germany
and Holland in 1433–4. Her husband had died in 1431, an
old man, and the last reference to Margery herself is in a
record of 1439.

Her autobiography as it has come down to us is in two
divisions or "books" of very unequal length, the first occupy-

[2] Extracts relating to Margery and her associates have been printed from the
records by Professor S. B. Meech and Miss H. E. Allen in their edition of *The
Book* (see last note), Appendix III, pp. 358–75. There is a chronological table of
her career, *ibid.*, xlviii–l.

ing 220 printed pages, while the second fills only fifty-four. Margery could not write herself, and the first book was written *c.* 1431, probably by her son who died in that year,[3] but written both illegibly and incomprehensibly, as the amanuensis, who had long lived in Germany, wrote in a mixture of two languages, without a mastery of either. The whole was re-written by a friendly priest under Margery's supervision in 1436, and in 1438 the shorter second book was composed, giving an account of Margery's Baltic tour and a few other incidents down to 1434.

The *Book of Margery Kempe* is thus utterly different in scope from the writings of Rolle, Hilton and the author of *The Cloud*. At first sight it might seem to have kinship with Julian's *Revelations*, for both books are strongly personal and purport to give the content of visions and locutions experienced by the narrator. Both might therefore fall into a general catalogue of literature under a single heading. The two books are, however, utterly different in character. With Julian a single series of visions, intimately connected with a single crisis in her spiritual life, is described at length and used for many years after as a collection of texts for reflections on theological mysteries and the relationship of the active and contemplative lives, and our interest, after the first few chapters, centres on the doctrines rather than on the person who is delivering them. With Margery Kempe, on the other hand, we have a detailed, though far from complete, survey of her life and activities over some forty years, and though visions and revelations make up a considerable part of the story from

[3] This identification was suggested to Miss Allen by Miss Joan Wake (*Book*, 258); against it, Miss Allen pointed out that the son was taken ill immediately on returning to England, and died after a month's illness. This, however, is not proof positive that he could not have acted as his mother's amanuensis; indeed the indecipherable handwriting and the confusion of language (cf. *Book*, 4/14–7; Butler-Bowdon, 346–7) might seem to strengthen the hypothesis of his having written the first draft.

start to finish, they do not, in any way perceptible to the reader, deepen the writer's spiritual insight or convey any message or programme to her readers. They are, almost entirely, devout conversations or monologues. Nor, it may be added, does Margery convey to the reader any of that sense of mental and emotional and spiritual distinction, and of that exceptional quality of personality, of which all readers of Julian's book speedily become aware. Margery Kempe is, in fact, a figure of a different kind, more homely, perhaps, and even more comprehensible, but of an altogether coarser mould.

The century divided by the year of Margery Kempe's birth (1325–1425) is from the hagiographical point of view distinguished by a remarkable series of women saints, several of whom were, or had been, married women, all of whom led lives of external movement in which the visionary and abnormal elements were strongly in evidence, and most of whom wrote accounts of their experiences. St Bridget of Sweden (d. 1373), St Catherine of Siena (d. 1380), St Katherine of Sweden (d. 1391), Bl. Dorothea of Prussia (d. 1394) and St Frances of Rome (d. 1440), are perhaps the best known, but there are many others, mostly of German or Dutch provenance.[4] Lynn, at this time at the height of its medieval prosperity, was one of the chief ports of communication with North Holland and the Baltic ports, while East Anglia was remarkable as the home of many recluses, men and women, and as the scene of the preaching and other spiritual activities of several of the most distinguished friars of the period. Margery Kempe was therefore almost ideally placed for the life of devotion; she had an abundance of potential directors and *conferenciers*, and she could readily acquire knowledge of

---

[4] Miss Allen (*Book*, lviii–lx, pp. 376–80 and *passim* in notes) gives many valuable suggestions as to sources of influence, promising a fuller and more methodical treatment in an "introduction" which has not yet appeared.

the lives and works of the holy women of Europe in the last generation. Though she was almost certainly unable to read, we know that her directors read to her frequently. She herself either mentions by name or quotes all the English mystics of our survey, and Miss Allen has indicated numerous similarities between her experiences, and her accounts of them, and those of her predecessors and contemporaries. These are so varied and so numerous that it is impossible to suppose that the resemblances are all purely coincidental, and doubtless many others will be discovered in the future.

The late Professor R. W. Chambers, in his preface to the first printed version of Margery Kempe's *Book*, likened her to the hotels which in older editions of Baedeker's guides were described as "variously judged",[5] and in the quarter-century that has elapsed since he wrote, his words have been repeatedly justified. Margery Kempe has been saluted by writers of repute as filling every rôle from that of saintly mystic to that of hysterical exhibitionist, while to some she has seemed to combine some of the qualities of both extremes. In her favour it must be noted that editors and most readers agree that her story gives an impression of basic sincerity. Margery may seem restless, talkative and self-centred, but she is at the same time a woman of faith and goodwill, charitable in word and deed; she never abuses her opponents and even suppresses their names, and she had among her advisers and supporters many whom we know from other sources to have been theologians and preachers of repute; when she can be checked, she is found accurate and truthful, and she displays courage, candour and good sense in many of her encounters with critics great and small. Against her may be urged the strong exhibitionist streak in her nature, and the absence of depth in the alleged spiritual communications. It is perhaps significant that the numerous marvels and visions

[5] *Margery Kempe*, 6.

and locutions, though never repellent and rarely silly, are the least striking part of her book; they give something of the same impression as do a series of banal conversations in an otherwise well-written novel of adventure. There is also the problem of reportage. Margery Kempe clearly had a remarkably good memory. Her first dictation took place at least thirty years after some of the events and reputed dialogues had taken place, and though it is noticeable that by far the greater part of the book is taken up with events that took place on her pilgrimages, long and short (and most readers will know that their own recollections of holidays and travels stand out with particular vividness), yet the detailed accuracy, which can often be controlled, is remarkable. Nevertheless, it is very hard to suppose that the long speeches of some of the celestial visitants, or even the more colloquial exchanges of the earthly characters, are in any sense direct reports of words heard or imagined at the time. Margery Kempe, indeed, would seem to be an early, if not the first, example in English prose literature of the skilful use of dramatically appropriate dialogue based on the substantial memory of what had taken place.

Two samples may perhaps show Margery at her best and on a lower level. The first is from a locution in her early life; it will be noticed that several phrases vividly recall passages of Julian, and may indeed be unconscious reminiscences of them:

> Then said our Lord in her mind: "I swear to thy mind, if it were possible for me to suffer pain again as I have done before, I would more readily suffer as much pain as ever I did for thy soul alone rather than that thou shouldst part from me for ever. . . . And though I withdraw sometimes the feeling of grace from thee, fear not therefore, for I am a hidden God within thee, so that thou shouldst have no vainglory and shouldst know well that thou mayst not have tears or speech but when

God will send them to thee, for they are the free gift of God
without thy merit, and he may give them to whom he will and
do thee no wrong. And therefore take them meekly and thank-
ingly when I send them, and suffer patiently when I withdraw
them, and seek busily till thou mayest get them, for tears of
compunction, devotion and compassion are the highest and
surest gifts that I give on earth. And what should I do more for
thee unless I took thy soul out of thy body and put it in heaven,
and that will I do not yet. Nevertheless wheresoever God is
heaven is, and God is in thy soul and many an angel is about
thy soul to keep it both night and day. For when thou goest to
church, I go with thee; when thou sittest at thy meat, I sit
with thee; when thou goest to thy bed, I go with thee; and
when thou goest out of town, I go with thee. Daughter, there
was never child so submissive to the father as I will be to thee
to help thee and to keep thee. I do sometimes with my grace as
I do with the sun. Sometimes thou knowest well the sun shines
all abroad that men may see it, and sometimes it is hidden under
a cloud that men may not see it, and yet is the sun never the
less in his heat and in his brightness. And right so do I by thee
and by my chosen souls.[6]

The second occurs shortly after the strange account of her
marriage to the Godhead in the church of the Holy Apostles
in Rome on 9 November, 1414:

She saw with her bodily eyes many white things flying all
about her on every side as thick as motes in a sunbeam. They
were minute and pleasant to see, and the brighter the sun shone,
the better could she see them. She saw them many different
times and in many different places, both in church and in her
room, at her meat and in her prayers, in field and in town, both
walking and sitting. And many times she was afeard what they
might be, for she saw them as well at night in darkness as in

[6] *Book*, 30/17–31/20; *Margery Kempe*, 349–50. This passage would seem to
show the influence of Julian (above, p. 130) and possibly also of both *The Cloud*
and Hilton.

daylight. Then, when she was afeard of them, our Lord said to her, "By this token, daughter, believe it is God that speaketh in thee, for wheresoever God is heaven is, and where God is there be many angels, and God is in thee and thou art in him. And therefore be not afeard, daughter, for these betoken that thou hast many angels about thee to keep thee both night and day that no devil shall have power over thee, nor evil man to harm thee." Then from that time forward she used to say when she saw them coming: "Benedictus qui venit in nomine Domini."

. . . Thys creature had divers tokens in her bodily hearing. One was a kind of sound as if it had been a pair of bellows blowing in her ear. She, being startled thereat, was warned in her soul to have no fear, for it was the sound of the Holy Ghost. And then our Lord turned that sound into the voice of a dove, and then he turned it into the voice of a little bird which is called a redbreast that sang full merrily ofttimes in her right ear.[7]

What is to be said of the alleged revelations and locutions? Were they genuine or real, even in the limited sense of being an inadequate way of receiving and expressing spiritual communications of any sort? Probably many of Margery's readers will feel that when the direct reminiscences of the writings and lives of other devout women, and the conscious elaboration of the dictating author have been allowed for, the balance must in most—perhaps in all—cases be credited to her very lively faculty of subconscious imagination. There existed quite clearly, and from the beginning of her adult life, a large hysterical element in Margery's personality, and the fluid and repetitive language and the insignificant content of many of the sayings attributed to Christ or to God the Father, and the prominent place taken in them by tributes to her excellence, contrast very strongly with the depth and sobriety of the *Dialogue* of St Catherine of Siena, the *Life* of

[7] *Book*, 88/6–25, 90/35–91/5; *Margery Kempe*, 353, 355.

St Teresa of Avila, and even with the *Revelations* of Julian of Norwich. In general, we may perhaps say that there is nothing in the words themselves that suggest any other origin than the vivid imagination and retentive memory of a sincere and devout, but very hysterical woman. To Margery it would seem that a careful passage of critical analysis in St John of the Cross might well be applied. He is describing various kinds of real or imaginary spiritual locutions, and dealing in particular with two classes of the latter. No abbreviation would do justice to the fine shades of meaning and delicacy of perception in his words.

These successive words come when the spirit is recollected and absorbed very attentively in some meditation, and in its reflections . . . it proceeds from one stage to another, forming words and arguments . . . with great facility . . . and discovering things . . . about the subject of its reflections, so that it seems not to be doing this itself, but rather it seems that another person is supplying the reasoning within its mind or answering its questions or teaching it. And in truth it has good cause for thinking this, for the soul itself is reasoning with itself and answering itself as though it were two persons conversing together; and in some ways this is really so; for although it is the spirit itself that works as an instrument in the case of genuine spiritual influence the Holy Spirit often aids it to produce and form these reasonings, words and conceptions . . . but inasmuch as this illumination which it receives is at times very subtle . . . so that the understanding cannot attain to a clear apprehension of it . . . it follows that the reasonings which it forms are frequently false. . . . And I am appalled at what often happens in these days . . . namely, when some soul with a ha'porth of experience, if it be conscious of certain locutions of this kind in some state of recollection, at once christens them all as coming from God, and assumes that this is the case, saying: "God said to me . . ."; "God answered me . . ."; whereas it is not so at all, but . . . it is for the most part they who are saying these things to themselves. There are certain types of understanding so quick . . . that they begin . . . to form their thoughts into the most lifelike words and arguments, which they think without any doubt come from God. Yet all the time they come only from the understanding which . . . is able to effect all this, and more, without any supernatural aid. This happens very commonly, and many persons are greatly deceived by it, thinking that they have attained to a high degree of prayer and are receiving communications from God, wherefore they either write them down or cause it to be written. And it turns out to be nothing, and to have the substance of no virtue, and it serves only to encourage them to vanity.

And the saint concludes:

Let us remember, then, this necessary caution . . . Let us treasure none of these things, but think only of learning to direct our will with determination to God, fulfilling His law and His holy counsels perfectly, which is the wisdom of the saints.[8]

If the *Book* of Margery Kempe has little in it of deep spiritual wisdom, and nothing of true mystical experience, it is a document of the highest value for the religious historian of the age. We see the towns of East Anglia well supplied with preachers and theologians ready to take an interest in, to advise, and often to expend considerable pains in helping and defending, anyone whom they considered to be deserving or unusually gifted. If some were repelled by the noise and disorder of Margery's "cryings", a majority, which included some of the most influential friars, were only too ready to accept her at her own valuation. Even the various prelates into whose presence she came treated her with considerable respect, particularly two who are not usually represented as spiritual men: Philip Repingdon of Lincoln and William Courtenay of Canterbury. What is perhaps more remarkable

[8] *Ascent of Mount Carmel* II xxix (Peers, I, 209–15).

still, in view of what we have seen of the teaching of the Dominican school and of the earlier English mystics, is that none of her counsellors made a serious attempt to develop her spiritual life on the lines laid down by Hilton—yet modern and even contemporary examples occur to mind of a similar failure on the part of a director to control or to eliminate what the masters of mystical theology agree in considering undesirable elements in one who wishes to advance in purity of life and prayer.

Among her many visits to spiritual persons for counsel or at least, to use her own term, for "dalliance", a particular interest attaches to that paid to Julian of Norwich in or about 1413 when the ancress was an old as well as a revered woman; this gives us the only contemporary evidence we possess of her life and personality outside the bare records. According to Margery, the ancress, "who was expert in such things and good counsel could give", accepted Margery's experience as genuine and her tears as authentic tokens of grace, but it seems clear that the visit took place before the "cryings and roarings" began, and the lengthy passage in *oratio recta* attributed to Julian in an account that was written down twenty years later is both theologically unexceptionable and remarkably vague, and might well represent the substance of advice given by a prudent woman who did not feel any obligation to overhaul the life of a passing visitor who was eccentric and self-centred if also sincere and devout.[9] It is to be noted that when Margery visited Norwich again two years later on her way back from Rome there is no mention of a visit to Julian.

In conclusion, it may be repeated that Margery Kempe can only improperly and accidentally be classed among the English mystics and that little of spiritual instruction is to be found in her *Book*, but she must in justice be credited with both moral and physical courage, and the readiness with which

[9] *Book* 42/7–43/20; *Margery Kempe*, 72–4.

she abandoned for the time her life of retirement to nurse and serve her ageing husband, after he had been disabled by a serious fall and had been reduced in his last years to helplessness, must weigh heavily in her favour in the final reckoning. The Wife of Lynn, with all her hysteria, is a more worthy and more sensitive woman than her older contemporary, the Wife of Bath.

Chapter IX

FATHER AUGUSTINE BAKER

WITH Julian of Norwich and Margery Kempe the succession of English medieval writers who, in one way or another, were concerned with the theory and practice of the contemplative life, came to an end. In this field, as in so many others, the remainder of the fifteenth century belied the promise of earlier years. This silence, however, was not due to any great revolution in contemporary religious sentiment or practice. Rolle and Hilton continued to be handbooks for the devout, both within and without the cloister, until the end of the reign of Henry VIII, and Hilton and the author of *The Cloud* continued during the same period to be the normal guides for those who were initiating themselves in the ways of prayer. At Syon Abbey and in the Charterhouses, in particular, the spirit of the English mystics continued to inform the spiritual *élite* of the country, though we can see, in the London Charterhouse and at Mount Grace priory, with such men as Nicholas Love and Richard Methley, that the somewhat different and more pietistic atmosphere of the later phases of the *devotio moderna* became a rival. Nevertheless, as the evidence of Carthusian book-lists and Short Title Catalogue of printed books, together with the researches of R. W. Chambers and Professor Dickens prove, *The Cloud* and its companions held the field till driven out by the full flood of the Reform, and were then carried into exile by more than one of the religious houses at the end of Mary's reign.

Even before the Reform had completed its conquests a

change had come in the currents of Catholic piety. While for the early Protestant reformers the mystical life in its traditional form held no attractions, in the Catholic camp also, throughout Europe, the need for a firm and explicit grasp of doctrine, and for an active, apostolic, sacramental, apologetic reply to opponents brought about a new model of the devout life which concentrated attention upon the war against vice and ignorance, and developed the technique of spiritual exercises, regular retreats, set meditations and methodical direction. The leaders of the Counter-Reformation, bent on reviving, instructing and organizing a Church about to go over from defence to the offensive amid wars and persecutions, naturally adopted the methods which the Jesuits in particular had perfected, and although in Spain the traditional contemplative life was entering upon a phase of unusual distinction with the mystical writers and saints of the Dominican, Franciscan, Augustinian and Carmelite orders, there was a lag of several decades before this movement reached the exiled English Catholics in France and the Low Countries. When, however, at the turn of the century, the older religious orders began to revive among the exiles, and in particular when the English Benedictine Congregation renewed its life with communities of men and women in what was truly a second spring of vigour, the English mystics became once more an influence, so that for a space of fifty years or so there was what may be regarded as a kind of prolongation, in a restricted field, of the spirituality of the fourteenth century. The originator and protagonist of what may almost be called the English school of spirituality in the last phase of the Counter-Reformation was Father Augustine Baker. His claim was excellently defined many years ago by Dom Justin McCann, to whom all are indebted for his work upon Baker's life and writings. "He is", wrote Dom Justin, "a striking, if not unique, figure in the history of post-

Reformation English Catholicism. The fourteenth century in England produced original spiritual writers of the first quality. If we look for any parallel to their work in post-Reformation Catholicism, we find one book, and one book only, Fr Baker's *Sancta Sophia*, which can be set beside it."[1] Indeed, we might go further still, and say that it is the only original work in English that gives magisterial guidance over a great part of the spiritual life. Whatever may be its limitations, or even its errors, it has the stamp of greatness. If Fr Baker is to be judged wanting, it is against the great that he must be measured, against such as St Francis de Sales, St Teresa and St John of the Cross.

During the past thirty years considerable attention has been paid to Father Baker, both as a spiritual writer of authority and as a principal agent in the rebirth of the English Benedictine Congregation, but no critical examination of his doctrine has yet been made, still less any thorough investigation of his own spiritual achievement. Indeed, despite the quantity of excellent work that has appeared, and the number of texts that have been made available, no attempt has been made to collate and examine all his voluminous writings, printed and unpublished, nor has a careful dissection and study been made of that great compendium of doctrine, *Holy Wisdom*. Yet both these pieces of work are absolutely essential as previous conditions of any definitive judgment on the man and his teaching. Here we are primarily concerned with the influence of the English Mystics on Father Baker and his school, but as Baker himself has some claim to the title of an English mystic in his own right, something must be said of his life and spiritual doctrine. For the historical

---

[1] *Memorials of Father Baker*, ed. R. H. Connolly and J. McCann (*Catholic Record Society*, XXXIII, 1933), introd. x. Several sections of this chapter have appeared in an article on Father Baker contributed to *The Clergy Review* of October, 1958, and I am grateful to the Editor for permission to reprint. I have, however, made a few not insignificant changes.

survey that follows reference has been constantly made to the remarkable store of biographical material recently made available in print through the enlightened industry of the late Abbot Justin McCann; the lives of Father Baker by his two disciples, Father Leander Prichard and Father Peter Salvin; the life written in the next generation by Father Serenus Cressy; and the accounts by Father Baker himself provided in his *Autobiography* (to 1596), his *Treatise of the English Mission*, and, above all, in the *Secretum* or commentary on *The Cloud of Unknowing* which contains a spiritual autobiography to 1629, extracted by Dom McCann and printed with the title of *Confessions of Father Baker*.[2]

David (in religion Augustine) Baker was born of well-to-do parents, church-papists, at Abergavenny in 1575 and had part of his schooling at Christ's Hospital and part at Broadgate Hall (now Pembroke College), Oxford, where, according to his own account, he lost his virtue and his Christian faith in bad company. He returned home, where he began a private study of the law which he completed in the Inner Temple from 1596. It was at this time, as we learn from his own account, that he was a not infrequent visitor to the theatre then (as he does not tell us) being rendered illustrious by the production of the central masterpieces of Shakespeare's art. During all this time his habit of irreligion continued, till he came to doubt the existence of God. He was recalled home by his father about the year 1599 and through

---

[2] Dom Justin McCann, himself a monk of the house of St Laurence to which Fr Baker belonged, but in which he never lived, devoted much of his scholarly life to presenting Fr Baker to our age. *The Confessions of Fr Baker* appeared in 1922, the *Lives of Fr Baker* by Fr Peter Salvin and Fr Serenus Cressy in 1933, and the autobiography, treatise on the English mission and *Life* by Fr Leander Prichard in the C.R.S. volume mentioned in the previous note. The account of Fr Baker's life that follows is drawn from his autobiography and the lives by Salvin and Prichard. Cressy's facts are derived from his predecessors, especially Prichard's *Life* "of which his own is often little more than a revised and shortened version" (McCann, *Lives of Father Baker*, xiii).

his influence became Recorder of Abergavenny; it was while engaged on business connected with this office that he had a strange and providential (as he thought) escape from death which aroused his sleeping faith and led gradually to his reconciliation to the Catholic Church, which took place in 1603 and was followed almost immediately by his departure to Italy to enter the noviciate of the celebrated Benedictine monastery of Santa Giustina at Padua. Here he entered upon a course of prayer, which he termed his "first conversion", but after three months fell into spiritual confusion and physical illness, and was advised to return to England, where he made his religious vows to English monks of the Italian Congregation who were on the mission, and took a leading part in the negotiations which led to the affiliation by Dom Sigebert Buckley of himself and others to the ancient abbey of Westminster, and later to the re-erection of the English Benedictine Congregation.[3] Meanwhile Dom Augustine, not yet a priest, retired into the country and embarked for a second time upon a life of recollection and prayer, his "second conversion", which he prosecuted with great earnestness (1608–9), attaining before long to an experience which in his own estimation marked an epoch in his life. To this we shall return later; here we need only remark that it was followed by a crisis of anxiety and aridity in which he once more abandoned prayer and returned to external activities and worldly company, practising the law. In 1610 he was ordained priest at Rheims. This for him unhappy state of things lasted for twelve years. Meanwhile, the negotiations for the formation of the English Congregation had come at last (1619) to a successful issue, and those already belonging to the group concerned were required to choose one of the three

[3] For a brief account of this, see J. McCann, *Ampleforth and its origins* (London, 1952), and the pages by the present writer in *The Religious Orders in England*, III, 445–56.

communities that had come into being in France and Lorraine. Fr Baker made choice of St Laurence at Dieulouard, but never in the event lived there. Instead, he accepted an offer of a post on the English mission in a remote part of Devonshire, where he lived as chaplain to the Fursden family. Here he began again with great earnestness a strict life of recollection and prayer, which he never again abandoned; this was his "third conversion", and he now began for the first time to act as spiritual director to others; it was the son of his host, later Dom Cuthbert Fursden, who, while living as chaplain to Lady Falkland, became acquainted with Hugh Cressy, who at one time acted as Anglican chaplain to her son, the celebrated Lucius Cary, and it was to Dom Cuthbert that Cressy attributed his conversion to the Catholic church.[4] After a year in Devon, Father Baker felt drawn to London, and removed thither, settling in the quiet of Gray's Inn, where he continued his life of recollection. It was at this period that he was given the task of investigating the history of the pre-Reformation Benedictines in England, a task that issued on the one hand in the *Apostolatus Benedictinorum in Anglia*, and on the other in the collection of a great mass of transcripts from medieval documents, many of which still remain in the possession of Jesus College, Oxford. While engaged in this work he made the acquaintance of several members of the distinguished group of antiquaries that contained Selden, Camden and Sir Robert Cotton; with the last-named, in particular, Fr Baker was on easy terms of friendship.[5] From this employment he was invited by his superiors

[4] A somewhat ambiguous phrase in Cressy's *Life of Fr Baker* (ed. McCann, p. 94), where a reference to Fr Cuthbert Fursden might superficially seem to apply to Fr Baker, has been taken, e.g. by the writer in the *Dict. Nat. Biog.* and by the present writer (*Religious Orders*, III, 456), to indicate Hugh Cressy's relationship of disciple to Fr Baker. The dates in Cressy's career (he was born in 1605) make this altogether impossible.

[5] A letter written by Fr Baker from Cambrai to Sir Robert Cotton, asking for copies of the works of English medieval spiritual writers for the nuns, is

to return to France, and within a few days of his arrival at St Gregory's, Douai, he was sent (1624) as auxiliary confessor to the newly founded community of English Benedictine dames at Cambrai. The nine years he spent there were in some respects the happiest and most fruitful of his life; he soon found himself as the spiritual director of a large part of the young and eager community starting upon their life in religion, and he composed for them a great number of spiritual treatises, including the *Secretum* containing his spiritual autobiography. It was then that he became well acquainted with the English mystics Rolle, Hilton and the author of *The Cloud*, and manuscripts exist, composed at this time, in which works of the two former are translated into contemporary English, while on the third he wrote a long and careful commentary. Trouble arose, however, between Father Baker and one of the official chaplains, Father Hull, and the orthodoxy of his doctrine was questioned. The controversy was at root one between a man of no great insight, who gave to his charges his version of the spiritual discipline of the Jesuit school, and the dedicated and scholarly Baker, who preached a simpler, more interior spirituality, but the issue was complicated by a difference of attitude in the two men towards liturgical and devotional practices in general, towards the functions of a spiritual director, and above all towards the characteristic Bakerian doctrine of "divine calls" or "inspirations". In the event, Fr Baker's teaching was formally vindicated by the superiors of the Congregation,[6] but both he and his adversary were removed from Cambrai, and Father Baker was called to St Gregory's at Douai. Here for the first time in his life he lived in a

preserved in the British Museum (MS Cott. Jul. C III f. 12) and is reproduced in facsimile in *Memorials of Father Baker*, facing p. 280. It was previously printed by H. Ellis, *Original Letters*, 2 ser., iii, 256–8.

[6] The official documents were printed at the end of earlier editions of *Sancta Sophia* (in the 1911 ed., entitled *Holy Wisdom*, pp. 551–4).

regular monastery, though his life was still a semi-eremitical one and he did not attend choir, but he continued his fruitful work as spiritual adviser, not only towards such of his brethren, and especially the younger ones, who came to him, but also towards other religious, clerics and laymen of the town, then the principal abode of the English Catholic exiles.

Once more, however, trouble arose. The young Congregation was divided between two parties, those of the English mission who extolled the dangers and glories of the apostolic work among heretics and (in some cases) enjoyed the freedom and social interests that such work could often bring, and those of the conventual party who held that the first duty of the English monks was to live the life of regular observance in the monastery abroad, and to take part in the theological and other controversies of the time. Father Baker had little sympathy with the shortcomings of the first class, and seems to have taken an unromantic attitude towards the dangers and inconveniences of the mission, which he had himself formerly shared, but in his zeal for solitude and prayer, he had almost as little enthusiasm for the leaders of the conventual party, and composed severe criticisms upon them, and especially upon the prior of his own monastery, the distinguished theologian Father Rudesind Barlow, who did not let the author go unpunished. In default of contemporary witnesses of acknowledged spiritual wisdom it is difficult for the historian to decide where principally the fault lay, and which of the parties was chiefly to blame. England, in the first half of the sixteenth century, had no lack of eminent men and powerful minds, but social tact, a spirit of compromise and tolerance, and a temper of wise good-humour are rarely evident in any field. To a superficial observer, Father Baker may seem an unaccommodating shipmate and Father Rudesind a ruthless superior, resolved to go to any lengths in ridding himself of a domestic critic. In any case, the

prior did not rest till he had secured a presidential order, over-
ruling a medical certificate, to send Father Baker, now elderly
and infirm, back to the mission in England. There he lived
for some three years, an invalid rather than a missioner,
harried about in 1640-1 by the agents of government in the
revived activity against Catholics, and escaping their hands
only by reason of a rumour of the plague in his house. He
died under the care of the mother of one of the nuns of
Cambrai in August, 1641.

This short narrative will have shown that there was little
of ordinary monastic observance in the external life of Father
Baker. For only five years, excluding the months of his
noviciate, was he the member of a community, and even
then, to judge from contemporary accounts, he was an *ex-
lex*. It may also have become clear that Father Baker was no
ordinary man. A gifted lawyer, who consorted on an equality
with the lawyers of a great age, a scholar who was admitted
to the circle of Selden, Cotton and Ussher, a tireless writer
who produced in the *Apostolatus* a laborious work of great
learning, and continued to pour forth tracts of every kind
upon the spiritual life, he undoubtedly deserves a place
among the distinguished men of a very remarkable period of
English history. Yet it is extremely difficult to form any
satisfactory judgment upon him as a man and as a spiritual
guide, and the deeper one goes in the literature about him,
the harder does the problem become. Three centuries after a
life has been lived, no one would wish to pose as a competent
judge of the finer shades of its significance, and the present
writer would not have opened the question had it not been
for the claims made in Father Baker's regard both in the past
and at the present day. He confesses that after more than
forty years' close acquaintance with *Sancta Sophia* he still
finds it difficult to assess "that mysterious man" who sits so
primly on his chair and gazes so sadly from the traditional

portrait. Father Baker is indeed a baffling figure. Powerful of
mind and determined of character, sane and central in all the
essentials of his doctrine, and able to influence his disciples
and contemporaries, not to speak of numberless readers since,
to their lasting good, he was clearly a good man, who did
good things. Yet he leaves upon us an impression of queer-
ness, as of a man with whimsies and corners;[7] a humourless
man, certainly not a "good community man", and he fell
seriously and perhaps needlessly foul of his confrères more
than once. Moreover, the autobiographical writings, and the
sketches of those who knew and revered him, confirm the
impression of an angular, even of a difficult man, unsocial,
untactful and self-centred, while some of his spiritual writings, though unquestionably orthodox, are on important
points confused and at variance with what would seem to be
the accepted doctrine of the great masters. These problems
will be resolved—if indeed they are susceptible of any resolu-
tion—only when a scholar with adequate theological preparation shall have read the whole corpus of Bakerian work, shall
have fitted it into the historical setting and spiritual climate
of the epoch, and shall have based upon it a comprehensive
and pondered judgment. A subsidiary question, however,
may and should be answered in the present book: was
Father Baker, in the strict theological sense of the term, a
mystic? That is, did he at any time meet with experiences
which would be considered fully mystical by an expert
theologian or director? The question is not without importance, for if answered in the affirmative, his teaching will
rightly be considered to possess an intrinsic authority; he will
be speaking of what he knows; he will have arrived, and his
directions to others will be trustworthy.

[7] Fr Salvin, indeed, loyally affirms that Fr Baker was "without crotchets"
(*Life*, p. 48). If crotchet is taken in its dictionary sense of mental crankiness,
perverse ideas, etc., this may pass, but Fr Baker's personal and social habits, as
related by Prichard, are queer in the extreme.

We must begin by acknowledging that his most intimate disciples considered him a mystic. Neither Father Prichard nor Father Salvin says so explicitly, but each makes it quite clear that this was his conviction. Father Serenus Cressy, who had no personal knowledge of him, is explicit in asserting that Father Baker attained to "passive union" in 1609–10 and that in his later life he was almost continually recollected in the prayer of "perfect active contemplation", and that on his deathbed he enjoyed "the greatest tastes of heaven that this life is capable of, his prayer being now become wholly passive".[8] None of these *Lives* was printed till recently, but Cressy's was preserved in several manuscripts, including four incorporated in the *Collections* of the congregational historian Benet Weldon, and it was familiar to Abbot N. Sweeney who, with his *Life and Spirit of Father Augustine Baker* (1861) and his edition of *Sancta Sophia* (1876) may be said to have introduced Father Baker to the modern world. Abbot Sweeney, in his introduction to *Sancta Sophia*, gives few details, but he commits himself to the statements that Father Baker's perseverance in prayer was "rewarded by ecstasies", and that Father Cressy was "his friend and disciple".[9] Subsequent writers, and in particular Abbot Cuthbert But-

[8] Cressy, *Life of Fr Baker*, 73–4, states: "He was brought to the supernatural prayer of proper aspirations, which is the prayer of perfect contemplation . . . certain most pure elevations proceeding from a divine impulse in the soul and flowing without any force at all." This is a fantasy of Cressy's which conflates "aspirations" = "infused acts of love" with the conception of "perfect contemplation". This last is a favourite Teresan term, taken by her probably from Bernardino de Laredo, and practically synonymous with contemplation *tout court*; for St Teresa it would seem to apply to the lowest degree of infused prayer. Cf. a series of articles, "Contemplative Prayer in St Teresa", by the present writer in *Downside Review*, LI, April, July, October, 1933. See especially no. 147 (July) 404–14. Cressy adds (p. 83) that at the end of his life "he was raised to a degree far higher than ever formerly he had attained to"—a statement that rests solely on his own interpretation of a phrase of Fr Baker's as reported by Prichard (see below, note 26).

[9] In Preface to *Sancta Sophia* (pp. x, xiv, ed. 1911). The latter phrase, as has been said, has misled several writers.

ler, have accepted Cressy's statements as reliable historical evidence, and have gone further to attribute to Father Baker himself all the mystical experiences described in *Sancta Sophia*.[10] As a natural consequence, others who have not studied the sources themselves have accepted Father Baker as a mystic, and even as an "eminent mystic". Yet if we consider the evidence a little more closely, we shall find that this reputation is derived solely and entirely from Fr Cressy's *Life*, and that Fr Cressy in his turn derives all that is not his own elaboration from the autobiographical details given by Fr Baker himself in the *Secretum* and from a message of his sent shortly before his death. What, then, is the testimony of the *Secretum* and this message?

We may begin by noting that in the *Secretum*, written at Cambrai in 1529, when Fr Baker was fifty-four years old and had already been five years with the nuns, there is only a single incident which could be considered (and was so considered by its author) as fully mystical, and that this had occurred twenty years previously and had been followed by a long interval of careless, or at least of unrecollected life. But in order to appreciate this incident, it is necessary to consider Fr Baker's scheme of the contemplative life as repeatedly given in the *Secretum* and never, to our knowledge, repudiated in after years. A fairly long quotation will probably be more helpful than any analysis:

> In the second place [that is, after "philosophic, natural contemplation"] there is mystic contemplation, which is indeed truly and properly such: by which a soul, without discoursings and curious speculations, without any perceptible use of the

[10] Abbot Butler, who, it is only fair to say, wrote before the *Lives* of Salvin and Prichard, and the *Confessions*, had been printed, does not stint his claims for Fr Baker, e.g. "a contemplative in the fullest and highest sense of the word, a rare mystic" (*Benedictine Monachism*, 1919, p. 104); "Father Baker's account [of the highest mystical union, *Sancta Sophia*, p. 533] was certainly based on personal experience" (*Western Mysticism*, 1922, p. 305).

internal senses or sensible images, by a pure, simple and reposeful operation of the mind, in the obscurity of faith, simply regards God as infinite and incomprehensible Verity, and with the whole bent of her will rests in Him as her infinite, universal and incomprehensible Good. This is true contemplation indeed.[11]

This passage, if the first two lines and the last sentence were omitted, would be an excellent description of the prayer, known to different writers as the prayer of faith, the prayer of simplicity, the prayer of simple regard, or the prayer of "acquired" contemplation, which in the scheme of St John of the Cross accompanies the night of sense, and which, as we know from other sources, the saint was in the habit of recommending to his Carmelite disciples when he was satisfied that they were capable of practising it. While it is not a prayer that any Christian of goodwill can practise at will, it is nevertheless not mystical, and St John more than once explicitly distinguishes it from "infused" prayer. Not so Father Baker, for he continues:

> This mystic contemplation or union is of two sorts: (1) Active and ordinary, being indeed an habitual state of perfect souls by which they are enabled, whensoever fit occasion shall be, to unite themselves actively and actually to God by efficacious, fervent, amorous and constant, yet withal silent and quiet elevations of the spirit.[12]

Here he conflates two essentially different species of prayer: the prayer of simplicity already mentioned, and the wholly infused prayer of love which is the true mystical prayer of contemplatives. He proceeds:

> (2) Passive and extraordinary: the which is not a state, but an actual grace and favour from God, by which He is pleased at certain times, according to His free good pleasure, to com-

[11] *The Confessions of Father Baker*, ed. J. McCann, 45.   [12] *Ibid.*, 46.

municate a glimpse of His Majesty to the spirits of His servants, after a secret and wonderful manner. And it is called passive, not that the soul therein doth not actively contemplate God; but she can neither when she pleases dispose herself thereto, nor yet refuse it when that God thinks good to operate after such a manner in the soul, and to represent Himself unto her by a divine particular image, not at all framed by the soul, but supernaturally infused into her. The which grace is seldom, if ever, afforded but to souls that have attained to the former state of perfect active union.[13]

Here again there is great confusion. Father Baker conflates once more two essentially different operations of God in the soul: true mystical, formless, knowledge, which alone is essentially contemplation, and particular illuminations or "revelations", which are inferior to, and essentially different from, that higher knowledge. Both are in the free gift of God, and neither can be directly merited or prepared for, but whereas the first, in perfect souls, is in its essence habitual, the latter is occasional and indeed ceases (in the form described in the above passage) in the fully mystical life.

Father Baker then recapitulates his doctrine:

Mystic contemplation is either active or passive. Of these two, active contemplation is . . . within the compass of all who dispose themselves to it . . . passive contemplation is no state, but a transient and brief experience. Therein is a special working of God above His ordinary course with men. . . . This happy state of active contemplation is for substance the most perfect that a soul is capable of in this life.[14]

Here again the same confusion reigns. Mystic active contemplation is a contradiction in terms; nothing mystical is within the compass of all who dispose themselves for it; passive contemplation is, if taken in the strict meaning of the term, another contradiction; if by passive is meant simply

[13] *Ibid.*, 46.   [14] *Ibid.*, 47.

infused, then it is not a transient, but an habitual, gift for perfect souls, if we understand by contemplation, not a particular
"revelation" but a formless, mystical knowledge. That Fr
Baker had no conception of the full mystical union, in which
the love and knowledge of the soul are both God's and the
soul's, is clear from numerous passages, as the following:

> [In passive union] certain species or images are infused by
> God into our souls, or He disposeth of the images that already
> are therein.[15]

And he is equally far from the truth when he writes:

> Our merit consisteth upon our own acts—though with the
> assistance of God's grace—and not the acts or doings where in
> God is the principal agent or only doer, and we but the
> patient.[16]

With this we may compare the doctrine of St John of the
Cross:

> This is the operation of the Holy Spirit in the soul that is
> transformed in love, that the acts which He performs within it
> . . . are most precious, and even one of them is of greater merit
> and worth than all that the soul may have done in its life apart
> from this transformation.[17]

Father Baker never grasps the great theological truth, that the
soul that has been enabled by the gift of God to rise
to the strength of giving itself wholly and really to God, and
to be moved freely by Him, is more truly the author of its
own actions (and therefore, if the word be used, more capable
of merit) than one which accomplishes with God's imperceptible help what it sees with its reason and faith to be
God's will.

Bearing in mind the doctrine of Father Baker as set out

[15] *Ibid.*, 62.   [16] *Ibid.*, 63.   [17] *Living Flame*, i, 3 (Peers, III, 119).

above, let us now approach the crucial incident of his life. He writes:

> And now as touching his passive contemplation [of 1608–9] itself he can say little in description of it, partly because it being a mere spiritual work it is not explicable in words, and partly for that now it is out of his and my memory [he is throughout writing of himself as of a "scholar" of his], being so many years since it was acted. But as far as memory now serveth I say that it was a speaking of God to the soul. I do not know whether the soul spake anything in answer to God or no. . . . As for the substance of it it is much out of his memory. This he then and yet knoweth with the greatest assurance that it cannot be but that it was the sole work of God and could not be the work of any creature. This he knoweth . . . by that that the work passed and was acted in the very substance of the soul, which could not be the work of any creature. Yet was it not a seeing of God.[18]

This might be thought to be a reliable, if somewhat jejune, description. Father Baker, however, goes on to give us the background:

> The said contemplation fell to our scholar in the forenoon, about eleven of the clock, and before he had eaten anything. He had—according to his wont—spent the forepart of that morning in his mental prayer that had been somewhat long and continued, and having give it over then the spirit of prayer came upon him—as it was wont to do—once or twice afterwards in that same morning. And the last time was a little before the said eleven of the clock, whereupon he was raised to the said contemplation. This I tell you that you may know my observation and opinion to be that such contemplation comes not usually on a man till after he has been long at his prayer and be come to the height of it, being so far and so high that he can go no farther nor no higher. And being come to such case God becometh the sole worker, as He is in all such passive contemplations; the which I suppose that they do not

[18] *Confessions*, 69.

come upon a man at the forepart of his prayer. I mean for his first passive contemplation. The same contemplation of our scholar lasted not, I think, above the space of half a quarter of an hour, or at the most but for one quarter of an hour. And it was with alienation from senses; I mean in a rapt.[19]

The reader must make what he can of this. Father Baker himself undoubtedly regarded it as an incident of unique significance in his life. Twenty years later he could write, in a passage of moving eloquence,

> It may well be, yea and most likely it will be—and that most justly and worthily—that God will deny our scholar the grace of a passive contemplation, in punishment of his neglect and ill-usage of his former passive contemplation, and will have him during his life to walk in and under the common light of faith and yet not to remain without some benefit of his former contemplation. The same contemplation is to put him in mind of his present poverty and darkness, and is to breed in him the more humility, indifferency and resignation, and make him the more careful hereafter to take heed of losing or decaying that which he had very dearly bought and lost as lightly and foolishly: bought with old gold and lost for an old song.[20]

We cannot fail to be reminded of that other experience, fifty years later, similar in some respects and problematic, yet far more vividly related—the night of fire of Blaise Pascal. Yet with Father Baker there is an element of strain and effort, and a singular lack of warmth, a preoccupation with his own efforts and feelings that are wholly lacking in the descriptions left us by the great mystics. With them the attention is concentrated on the Person, the Love, the Truth they have encountered. Of this, there is nothing in Father Baker's words. Whatever he may have experienced, it was not the mystical union of the soul with God. Indeed, when we have the whole context before us, and remember the subsequent rapid loss of

[19] *Ibid.*, 60–1.   [20] *Ibid.*, 149.

spiritual energy, it is difficult to see in the incident anything more than an abnormally vivid process of thought in a mind exhausted by effort and perhaps also by physiological fatigue.

The reader may consider this a harsh and insensitive judgment, but he must take into account the strange description that Father Baker gives to his young penitents at Cambrai of the physical accompaniments of his prayer at the time of writing:

> It seemed to him that his soul did work and exercise them [sc. his "aspirations"] forth and without the body, ... here and there, up and down; but all of them seemed to be without the doors or windows of the body. Afterward [a year and a half later] it seemed to him that his working came to draw towards and into the body. And first they came to the extreme parts of it, as into the hands and feet, and afterwards into the arms and legs ... by little and little drawing towards the middle part of the body, as the breast, etc., ... and this exercise about the middle part of the body continued about the space of a year; and therehence by little and little the working went upwards and came into the neck, and thence went higher into the head, and it seemed to him that it brake forth in his eyes, so that he thought that if any man had well regarded his eyes he must note some alteration in them.[21]

His eyes, however, he remarks, had no strange appearance, for his exercise proceeded from the spirit, whereas staring of the eyes and giddiness of the head "is usually noted in them who use much and long meditation ... and namely [i.e. especially] those that are in or newly come forth out of those exercises that are usually termed to be spiritual exercises, that are ministered by the Fathers of the Society of Jesus and some others".[22] As for his own experience,

> It seemeth to me that our scholar's exercise of the will tended upwards and by a consequence drew with it or after it what was

[21] *Ibid.*, 94–6.   [22] *Ibid.*, 96–7.

beneath. His labour in it, albeit it were much the lighter, having in it such a helper and mover as he had [Fr Baker presumably means the Holy Spirit] yet it was not without some pain or difficulty to nature, especially in regard the work continued sometimes, yea, frequently, long, as for five, six, or seven hours' space in the forenoon; so that in the time of the said working there seemed to be, at the first about the breast or middle part of the body and afterwards about his head, more heat and warmth than was about the extreme parts of the body. So that, even in some of the cold seasons of the year, lying in bed he could endure over his body but only a linen sheet, and no other covering, and nothing—I mean no night-cap, which he used at all times—on his head; and this, I mean, was while lying in his bed he was in the said working exercise of his. In the said exercise of his there was both pain and difficulty, and yet withal there was a facility. . . . Albeit I told you that his exercise about the breast was without corporal motion, yet was not the previous exercise that I said to have been in hands, arms, feet and legs, altogether without motion. For half a year to-gether his evening's exercise (not his morning's) had those motions in them, and certain senseless aspirations were joined with those motions, and the motions were very strong and violent. . . . Our scholar living alone was and might be loud enough in his voice, uttering and venting forth his foresaid senseless aspirations, yet not so but that he was sometimes in peril to have been heard by others, and if he had been heard or seen he would doubtless have been adjudged for a man that were out of his wits.[23]

Then, as a warning to his young nuns, he continues:

Let them that are moved with sensible devotion take heed that they do not mistake their case, resembling it to the cor-poral motions of our foresaid scholar, for there is a great differ-ence between them. For the sensible devotion that beginneth in the body or in the senses of it, (as doth all sensible devotion

[23] *Ibid.*, 99–100; 101–2.

of beginners) is neither so profitable to the soul, nor so free from danger to health and from diabolical illusions, as that corporal or sensible devotion that beginneth in spirit and thence descendeth into the body, as did the foresaid corporal or sensible devotion of our scholar.[24]

This long extract may well leave us uncertain whether to wonder at the painful sincerity of the writer more than at the entire absence of any spiritual content; and our wonder is not lessened when we notice that he applies to his own strange antics the teaching of the great mystics on the experience of souls of great purity.

The assertion of Father Cressy, that in the last year of his life Father Baker was almost continually recollected in the prayer of "perfect active contemplation", means very little. The phrase he uses, in itself a contradiction in terms, is based on Fr Baker's own definition already quoted which, as has been seen, conflates two distinct degrees of prayer and certainly does not refer to the higher of these. It is, in any case, as described both by Fr Baker and by his first biographers, not a mystical prayer,[25] and however much we may respect Fr Baker's devotion and faith, perseverance in prayer cannot by itself justify us in ranking him among the mystics.

As regards his state of prayer during his last illness we have the evidence of Fr Prichard:

He bad me let them [sc. the dames at Cambrai] know "that he was now *totus in passionibus*"; and "that one dram of suffering was worth more than a hundred pounds of doing". And I remember, I wrote so to Cambrai. But yet I was very desirous to know of him, what he meant by being *totus in passionibus*; for I knew he did not suffer by any persecution, nor wants, etc.,

---

[24] *Ibid.*, 102–3. Cf. St John of the Cross, *Ascent*, ii, §1 (Peers, I, 102).

[25] *Confessions*, 120: "And you must know that the highest of our scholar's contemplations since his last conversion hath been but an active contemplation and not a passive."

having so good a nurse; and yet on the other side, I wondered if his praier or contemplation were wholly passive. But by another letter from him, I was confirmed in the truth of this latter.[26]

On this we may note; first, that it is the only evidence on the matter, and that the embroideries of Fr Cressy, as well as the notices of subsequent writers down to Abbot Butler, are based upon this alone. Secondly, Fr Prichard, though clearly a sincere and truthful reporter, was an ardent disciple, not to say a partisan, of Fr Baker and his spirituality, and that we have no evidence, either from his own writings or from any other source, that he was qualified either by theological training or by personal experience, to make a critical judgment upon supernatural states of prayer. Nor does he quote the exact words of Fr Baker. Two separate questions need an affirmative answer: Did Fr Baker in his ambiguous phrase claim a fully mystical experience of a higher kind than any save the half-hour at Cookhill thirty-five years earlier? And, if so, did he imply by this claim what St Teresa or St John of the Cross, or, for the matter of that, Walter Hilton would have accepted as fully supernatural contemplation? It is hard to see how, with what we have to go upon and with our lack of full knowledge, we can give a clear and affirmative answer. On a matter of such delicacy and weight, only the unambiguous language of trustworthy personal statement, or the declaration of a fully qualified witness such as, for example, Domingo Bañez in the case of St Teresa, can be accepted as probative. That Fr Baker died the death of a just man after a life of great spiritual worth is of course not in question, but

[26] *Life* by Fr Leander Prichard in Memorials, p. 152. According to Fr Cressy, Fr Baker's last message was: "Abstinence and Resignation I see must be my condition, to my very expiration" (*Life*, p. 139). There is a strange absence of any explicit reference to a "personal" love of Our Lord in these documents on Fr Baker's spirituality.

whatever may or may not have been his experiences in the last days of his life in London, they cannot alter the fact that he claimed nothing of the kind between 1608 and 1642. It is instructive to compare his writings and life with those of Fr Constantine Barbanson, whom he quotes so readily. The reader inevitably perceives that Barbanson is describing what he himself has experienced, and is describing it in correct theological language, and the accounts of contemporaries bear witness that this impression is justified.[27]

Yet whatever we may think of passages such as have been cited above, they must not be allowed to blind us to the clarity and wisdom that Father Baker almost invariably shows when writing, not for publication, for of that he did not dream, but for careful and methodical instruction. Indeed, the very Commentary on *The Cloud*, of which the autobiographical passages are a part, is excellent in its precision of analysis and in the sound sense of its instruction. But what has been quoted may at least make us pause before attributing to the writer the competence that comes from personal experience in the high things of the spirit.

Father Baker, lawyer, scholar and spiritual director, was a voluminous writer. Indeed, "penning", as he called it, was a daily occupation with him on a level with reading and praying. In addition to the *Apostolatus*, four folio volumes of material for monastic history, two autobiographical pieces, a short history of the origins of the English Congregation, lives of Dame Gertrude More and one or two others, and a commentary on the *Cloud of Unknowing*, he left numerous treatises on various ascetical and mystical topics. It was chiefly from these last that a monk of the next generation, himself a

[27] Dom J. McCann, who edited *The Secret Paths of Divine Love* (London, 1928), tells us that the author, after an apostolic life, died "in the fullest odour of sanctity" (p. xi) and remarks with justice: "Father Constantine obviously writes of that which he had himself experienced; there is no other explanation of his book."

distinguished Oxford man and convert, Dom Serenus Cressy, compiled, at the request of the dames of Cambrai and with the warm support of his superiors, the book which he entitled *Sancta Sophia* or *Holy Wisdom*.

Anyone who has glanced at only one of Fr Baker's manuscripts will feel that Fr Cressy achieved a notable feat of editing. He has indeed, to use his own phrase, "methodically digested" Fr Baker's remains and produced an ordered whole, and what appears as a system, out of disconnected and prolix treatises. Nevertheless the method has its disadvantages. Until someone has worked through the existing manuscripts and analysed their contents, we cannot be sure that Fr Cressy has given us the whole of Fr Baker's teaching, and until the relevant passages have been collated with *Sancta Sophia* we cannot be sure that the order and arrangement of the parts fully corresponds to Fr Baker's scheme. Fr Cressy, in short, may have considerably modified the doctrine, for better or for worse. Meanwhile, and in particular for present purposes, we have to take *Sancta Sophia* as we find it, and equate the printed book with Fr Baker's mind.

If Fr Cressy compiled his work out of Fr Baker's treatises, whence did Fr Baker himself derive his doctrine? We may begin with some negative remarks. Fr Baker had not passed through an academic or seminary course of philosophy and theology, and though he had read, as we shall see, some scholastic authors he never writes as a trained theologian, either explicitly, as did, for example, his Carmelite contemporaries at Salamanca or John of St Thomas, or implicitly, as did St John of the Cross. This absence of theological backbone is one of the weaknesses of *Sancta Sophia* and, indeed, of all Fr Baker's compositions. Next, Fr Baker, as has been said, never lived the community life of an observant monastery at any time after his half-noviciate at Santa Giustina. His counsels for religious, therefore, were not the outcome of long experience of the common life, or of the responsibilities of office.

If we now come to the positive influences, we may say that *Sancta Sophia* rests upon Fr Baker's experience, personal and vicarious, and upon his reading. His personal experience, though he never cites it, lies behind many pages, as may readily be seen by comparing one of the personal treatises, such as the printed *Confessions*, with the relevant sections in the book. Yet he may well have learnt most from his own disciples. In his years at Cambrai he found a door open and, though even here he held no official position of superiority, he was able to use his exceptional gifts in forming and direct-ing a young community of zealous and gifted women. In return he unquestionably learnt much of human nature and the ways of God in calling a soul to Himself. When we esti-mate the extent of his debt to the nuns of Cambrai, however, we must remember that when he arrived at the convent all the nuns were "beginners" in the spiritual life, and though one at least, Dame Gertrude More, advanced towards per-fection in the short span allotted to her, the community of Cambrai in those first years cannot be compared to the galaxy of spiritual talent that St John of the Cross knew at Beas and Granada, or that St Francis de Sales fostered in the house by the lake at Annecy.

And when all has been said, Fr Baker owed the basis of his teaching to books. He was a scholar rather than practitioner, and there is abundant evidence, which an editor must some day display, of the breadth of his reading and of his debt to his books. The decades of his maturity coincided with the first great wave of what Bremond has called *l'invasion mystique*, when the books and first disciples of the great Spanish and Italian saints were arriving in France and the Low Countries to kindle new fires and light new lamps there. Of this invasion Fr Baker was at once a beneficiary and an agent. His sources were many and remarkably well chosen. In the first place, he had the *Conferences* of Cassian and the *Lives of the Fathers*, recently popularized by Rosweyde. From the early Middle Ages he took something from St Anselm, St Bernard and William of St Thierry. He read the *Summa* of St Thomas carefully, and knew the spiritual writings of St Bonaventure. From a later century he took something from St Catherine of Siena and Blessed Angela of Foligno. Two of the English mystics, the author of *The Cloud* and Walter Hilton, were among his favourite authors; he wrote a commentary on the former and advised his nuns to read the book yearly. Of the Swiss and Flemish mystics he knew parts of Ruysbroeck and Suso, and of Germans Tauler, Ludolf the Carthusian and above all Herp (Harphius). Of the Spaniards he cites Osuna and Alvarez de Paz, but these are naturally outweighed by St Teresa (canonized in 1622) and St John of the Cross (not yet beatified); he seems, however, to have been familiar only with the *Ascent* of St John and the *Life* and *Interior Castle* of St Teresa, though both writers had been translated into French in quasi-totality. In consequence, and perhaps unfortunately, he treats them eclectically as supporting authorities without adopting in its entirety the Carmelite mystical theology, perfected by St John, as a regulative norm, and he displays no acquaintance with the Carmelite theologians of Salamanca or the great Dominican theologian John of St Thomas. Among the writers of his own day, his favourites were the two Franciscans, Constantine Barbanson and Benet Canfield, but he knew the *Introduction to the Devout Life* of "the holy bishop of Geneva", the works of Blosius, and several of the Jesuit writers. From all these, but principally from Tauler, Harphius, Suso, *The Cloud*, Barbanson and Canfield he distilled his doctrine, and it is not surprising that the result, which he himself never fused into a system, has a patchwork appearance. He rarely argues from theological principles; the reason given is the opinion of an authority, though it is often critically examined. He never fully adopts the system of any one authority: thus he frequently quotes *The Cloud* and Barbanson (who agree in essentials), yet takes up positions directly contrary to theirs. There are indeed passages of fire and eloquence, which a reader would suppose to be the utterances of experience, but certain of these, at least, can be shown to be precisely those where he is following a printed source.

Sancta Sophia is a carefully arranged series of instructions for one engaged upon the religious life, and especially the "monastical contemplative life", and it aims at covering every stage from the first entrance of the postulant to the mystical union of perfect souls. It is therefore a treatise of both ascetical and mystical theology, though the strictly mystical teaching occupies only fifty out of five hundred pages. No other book is exactly comparable; it stands half-way between a set and formal treatise of ascetical theology and a loosely knit, personal instruction such as is given by St Teresa in her *Way of Perfection*; more comprehensive and orderly than the latter, it is more direct personal and urgent than the former. It is indeed one of the very few spiritual masterpieces that can be read again and again, and serve as a life's support. The late Abbot Cuthbert Butler read it at least once a year for more than fifty years on end. It is, however, an unusually difficult book to summarize, for despite the efforts of Fr Cressy's "methodical digestion" it remains a heap rather than a block or a building, and there are chapters, valuable and indeed of themselves indispensable, which cannot be pressed into any logical order and could be excised without leaving a chasm.

Partly of its very nature and partly because of its author's slant of mind, *Sancta Sophia* may also be considered as a guide to prayer. Its subtitle, indeed, is "Directions for the prayer of contemplation". Its scope, however, is really very much wider and yet much less complete than this. It is divided by Fr Cressy into three treatises: (1) of a contemplative life in general; (2) of the first instrument of perfection, viz., mortification; and (3) of prayer; but these headings give no idea of the richness of the whole. After general instructions on the religious life, three particular means of internal enlightenment are discussed: the spiritual director, spiritual reading and divine inspirations. Then, after sections on the obligations of the religious life, on the noviciate and on the English mission, the author deals with the mortification of the passions and the practice of solitude and silence; then with the virtues of charity, patience, humility and obedience, after which comes a long chapter on the treatment of scruples. All this takes up some 330 pages. The 220 pages that remain are occupied with prayer: the manner of using sensible devotion and distractions; a full treatment of the three stages of meditation, acts of the will and "aspirations"; instructions for behaviour in distractive offices and in sickness. Finally, an outline, a very jejune outline, is given of the stages of the mystical life.

Father Baker is diffuse and at times verbose, but he had a capacious and masculine intelligence, and the book is dense with the reading and experience of many years. Before discussing it a word of caution may be in place. Like other spiritual classics, such as *The Cloud of Unknowing* and the writings of St Teresa and St John of the Cross, *Sancta Sophia* was composed for a restricted class of readers and will only be read with real profit by those belonging to that class. While it is true that all the books just mentioned may prove of interest, and even incidentally of help, to the casual reader, they were in fact composed for those already committed to a strict religious life and they contain some matter, at least, which can be easily misunderstood by those in other circumstances. In *Sancta Sophia*, indeed, the appeal is wide and the danger of misunderstanding less. It is nevertheless true that the book will prove of real use and value only to a soul committed, or desirous of being committed, to a resolute endeavour to advance in the love of God in an "abstracted" way of life. As Fr Leander of St Martin wrote of Fr Baker's doctrine in 1634, it is "written precisely and only for such souls as by God's holy Grace do effectually and constantly dedicate themselves to as pure an abstraction from creatures . . . and all things which they shall perceive, or be warned of, to be impediments to the divine union of their souls with God"[28] as may be possible, and others will read *Sancta Sophia* at their own hazard.

Having said thus much, it must be added that the doctrine and the manner of presentation throughout the book are sobriety itself. On a multitude of ascetical topics Fr Baker gives, with clarity and authority, the central teaching of the masters of the spiritual life throughout the ages. Indeed, if he errs at all in this respect, it is on the side of authority and convention. Nothing in his teaching could be interpreted in an extravagant sense save by a perverse or extremely stupid reader. With this preface, something may be said about three points in Fr Baker's teaching which are of particular value: on mortification, on divine inspiration and on the first degrees of mental prayer.

As to mortification, or the ascetic life, he is at once simple and bracing, granted always, what he assumes, that the person concerned is living under a firm rule of life. He may be summed up, positively, as finding mortification of the passions in a strict observance of the Rule and religious obedience, and, negatively, in the avoidance of all distraction of the mind and squandering of the will, and in the practice of solitude, silence and the renunciation of all activity that results from free, personal choice. More explicitly, perhaps,

[28] *Sancta Sophia*, 535.

than any other writer he insists upon the avoidance of all "propriety", that is, the enjoyment of a sense of possession, power or achievement, whether in regard to things, persons or employments; and upon the value of not-doing rather than doing. Here he is absolutely at one with the Carmelite school as expressed by St John. On the other hand, he discounts the value of purely physical mortifications, and especially of all such as are voluntarily and hastily assumed. Nor is he afraid to say that prayer, the kind of prayer he extols, is the best of all mortifications.

As for his teaching on divine inspiration, it is perhaps the most original and valuable part of his work. Many are the souls that have profited and will profit by it, properly understood and practised, and many are those to whom it might bring comfort and strength. It is not, of course, original in the sense of novel, for Christian spirituality has been essentially the same in every age. Not only this, but many writers, from the Fathers of the desert onwards, have given explicit instruction on this very point. It had, however, become obscured in the decay before the Reformation and in the authoritarian climate of the early sixteenth century, and its revival in a heretical and deformed sense had made it something of an unwelcome topic to the spiritual writers of the Counter-Reformation. Yet it may be said that without it there can be no mature and truly strong life of the spirit. The teaching, which is in fact universal Christian teaching applied to a particular point, is that in all cases and on all occasions where a moral or spiritual decision has to be taken, and where no clear law or command makes the will of God here and now apparent, light to see (and strength to act) will be given without fail to one who asks for it with faith and goodwill. The doctrine, it must be repeated, has its fullest relevance only for souls aiming at the highest. Christians who are in and of the world, and even many priests and religious, have not in fact and in the concrete case either the desire or the spiritual capacity to follow the inner light in the "ordinary" decisions of life. But for those who wish to hear and respond to the call to a more perfect following of Christ the doctrine is essential. Those who are honest with themselves will know that the turning points, the crucial decisions for good and bad throughout their lives, have not occurred on a matter of law or expressed command, but in the intimate and unseen region of the soul where the gift or the refusal of the will to God and of love to Christ takes place. How often, if we have any knowledge of ourselves, are we aware that a vital opportunity has been lost precisely because the very existence of a moment of choice has been burked, or, if the opportunity has been taken, that the decision has been made under the guidance of an unseen but intimately experienced illumination! Every sincere Christian knows, on his humble level, what is writ large in the lives of the saints—in St John of the Cross, who wrote:

> Unseeing, on I pressed
> Lit by no earthly rays,
> Nay, only by heart's inmost fire ablaze,

and St Thérèse of Lisieux, of whom the Church sings: "the Lord alone was her guide".

Finally, there is Fr Baker's teaching on the necessity and stages of mental prayer. This is the heart of his book, and its "message" for his generation and for ours. He belonged, as has been said, to the age-group that came to maturity when the writings and exhortations of the saints and leaders of the Catholic Reform were permeating Europe and germinating luxuriantly into flower and fruit, as also into coarse herbage and hybrid growths. Broadly speaking, the spiritual reform had taken two directions. There was the efflorescence of intellectual, pastoral and missionary activity—the new education, the Jesuit colleges, the discipline of preaching, retreats and meditation, the renewed frequentation of the sacraments. There was on the other hand a revival of the strict religious and contemplative vocation, accompanied by the appearance of a constellation of saintly men and women who by their example and writings infused new blood into the traditional mystical theology of the Church. The revived English monasticism of men and women, of which Fr Baker had been an active pioneer, was drawn by opposing magnets. On the one hand were the new colleges, the methodical asceticism, the preaching and directing, and the call of souls on the English mission; on the other, the tradition of the monastic past and the vision of the heights of Mount Carmel. Father Baker had felt the struggle in himself and seen it in the controversies within his own monastic family and in the arguments even within the parlours of the English dames. He saw it as his vocation to preach and to present the cause of the interior life and of mental and contemplative prayer. For the moment the controversial element in his life can be ignored; for us he is the apostle of the prayer of the spirit. Here, he does but return to the purest sources of monastic and mystical doctrine, the desert Fathers, who saw in the prayer of the heart, the prayer of love and adoration, the end of the monastic life and the inseparable companion of all true virtue. But Fr Baker, in emphasis at least, goes even further; for him mental prayer is the centre and the test of all. Neither in his own practice nor in his teaching does he neglect or belittle the sacraments, or the liturgy, as instruments and sources of sanctification, but he is insistent that the monk must be a man of interior prayer, and that only so far as he is a man of prayer, or needs help to make him a man of prayer, are other things of value. As he remarks very truly, the prayer of the heart and will is the only activity incompatible with deliberate sin. The sacraments may be received mechanically or unworthily, vocal prayers may be said with every kind of mental preoccupation, but humble and sincere interior prayer—the explicit or implicit *fiat voluntas tua*—is not compatible with an actual resistance to God's will and love.

In his account of the degrees of prayer Fr Baker, who is writing, be it remembered, for those dedicated to a monastic life, passes rapidly over formal meditation. This, in his view, should never, for the monk or nun of an enclosed order, be more than a short stage, while for some it should not be a stage at all. For those for whom he is writing, liturgy and meditative reading, both part of their daily life, should take the place of meditation in feeding the mind for as long as it needs to find motives for love. For the monk prayer should become immediately and solely an activity of the will, loving, praising God, accepting His will in all things and trusting in His light and help. It is the great merit of Fr Baker that by his description and by the examples he provides he shows the richness, the potentialities and the stages of growing purity in this kind of prayer. Many readers of Fr Baker will of course find, like the would-be literary man of Molière, that they have in fact long been practising something of which they now learn the technical name, but there may be others to whom a chapter of Fr Baker will come as an open door and a new freedom.

Thus far we have laid emphasis upon the excellencies of Fr Baker. A word must now be said of his deficiencies. Such criticisms as follow, it must be remembered, apply primarily to the printed *Sancta Sophia* but they have regard also to his *Confessions* and other published writings.

The first criticism is a general and not a very serious one. *Sancta Sophia* is a long book and it would not have lost a great deal if Fr Cressy had been somewhat more ruthless with the pruning-knife. Moreover it is, at least in its first half, a somewhat sombre book. Father Baker himself was, so we are told, approachable and sympathetic, especially in his relations with the young, but he lived in a mental climate heavily charged with a dour view of human nature deriving partly from the preoccupation of theologians with the treatises of St Augustine on grace, and partly from the influence of Calvinism and Puritanism on contemporary religious sentiment. There is more than a foretaste in Fr Baker of the sunless outlook of Saint-Cyran and Port-Royal. Three or four passages, indeed, seem to exclude the possibility of "natural" moral goodness and to contradict both Catholic teaching and common experience in attributing actual sinfulness to all love that is not actually or virtually directed towards God.[29]

More serious, perhaps, is a real confusion in the degrees of the spiritual life and the principles of mystical theology, even if, as is possible, some of the confusion may be due to Fr Cressy's arrangement of the chapters. Put briefly, it would seem that Fr Baker failed to arrive at an adequate definition of contemplation. As has been said, he had read some, though not all, of St John of the Cross, but he had failed altogether to absorb and make use of two of the basic principles of the teaching which the saint drew from earlier tradition and which have since become the common doctrine of theologians. The one is, that no clearly expressible knowledge and no clearly felt emotion or effort in the will can be a proximate means of union with God: the only proximate means are the virtues of faith in the intellect and of hope and charity in the will. The other is, that normally perfection of the soul cannot be attained without passive purgation of the intellect and will by means of God-sent darkness and aridity, which are in fact the impact upon an imperfect being of divine light and love. Hence the need for the twofold purification of sense and spirit in the two "nights" within the soul. Without this clear

[29] E.g. pp. 200–1, 230, 245, 249–50, 251.

position, based firmly on the traditional theology of grace and of the functions of the theological virtues and the gifts of the Holy Ghost, Fr Baker had to find his way amid a tangle of schemes based largely on individual experience, his own and that of others. Several serious inconveniences resulted from this.

First, Fr Baker, who was well aware of the elementary part played by the imagination and the reason in prayer, failed to see clearly that in the realm of the will his "forced acts" were equally elementary. Both are activities belonging to the stage of "meditation". Father Baker, therefore, is at fault when he describes the prayer of the will, *tout court*, as "contemplative", and also when he places his instructions on the season for a change of prayer between the section on meditation and that on acts of the will. The crucial moment of transition is when both "considerations" and formal "acts" are beginning to give place to the prayer of simplicity or loving attention which precedes the reception of infused love and knowledge. The confusion may have been in part caused by the scheme of St John himself in *The Ascent of Mount Carmel*. There, the saint places the crucial line of division at the moment of abandoning "meditation" because he is treating of the night of the understanding. When he comes to deal with the night of the will he does not in fact discuss the point again, but it is clear from many other allusions that he would there have drawn the line at the moment of abandoning express "acts". Common experience corrects Fr Baker. The decision to abandon set meditation can be made very early in a spiritual course by principles of good sense; the other decision is far more serious, demanding true spiritual discretion, and it occurs normally at a real crisis in the soul's growth.

Having once made this initial mistake Fr Baker is drawn into another. Having labelled the prayer of forced acts "contemplative" he is compelled to make the limits of this prayer very extensive, ranging through every degree of increased purity up to what he calls a "passive union"; to clarify matters he makes within it a higher division which he labels "aspirations", in his terms but not in his spirit following Fr Benet Canfield. This arrangement leads him inevitably to a subdivision of contemplation into "active" and "passive" which not only runs counter to the dictum of St John and other great mystical theologians, including as we have seen the English mystics, that "contemplation is to receive",[30] but also leaves no place for the division of classical mystical theology between the human and supernatural "modes" of acting; and between "operant" and "co-operant" grace, which we have seen so clearly enunciated in *The Cloud* and *The Scale*. Actually, Fr Baker's "aspirations" include two theologically distinct forms of prayer, the one a simplified and elevated form of "acts of the will" and the other an infused prayer. He thus omits entirely (save in a not very satisfactory intercalated chapter)[31] any mention of the true "intermediate" prayer, the so-called "prayer of simple regard", the "acquired contemplation" of many spiritual writers, of which there are several passing hints in St John's treatises and which he is known in practice to have taught to his novices. It is this fundamentally unreal treatment of contemplative prayer that confirms the historian's doubts that Fr Baker himself had any experience of the mystical life.

Finally, the reader wonders now and then whether Fr Baker, in his flight from the mechanical and artificial "spirituality" of some of the "active livers" with whom he was brought into contact, has not fallen into a Charybdis of his own, by making prayer as an exercise, a pursuit, an effort, almost a life, into something with a mechanical efficacy of its own, the one clue and talisman. When all is said, the sole true

[30] *Living Flame* III §36 (Peers III 180).
[31] Third Treatise, Section III, Chap. vii.

end of the soul's life is to be united in will with God through love of Him and one's neighbour—prayer it is, no doubt, in the deepest, simplest sense, but not prayer as an effort or activity distinguished from other virtues or activities of the Christian life.

These flaws in Fr Baker's teaching, if they are really such, must detract from the value of *Sancta Sophia* as a manual of mystical theology and advanced contemplative prayer. They do not, however, seriously affect its value for the "discreet, well-minded soul", the "internal liver" for whom it was so laboriously composed. Such confusion as may exist does not affect at all the practical instruction of the first three-quarters of the book, in which its greatest value consists. A soul well established on this basis, and with a sane liberty of spirit, will be directed to other guides, such as the great Carmelite saints, or will be enabled to follow, without book-learning, the guidance of the Holy Spirit. Moreover, Fr Baker is not, so to say, a logical heretic, or even consistent in his definition. Alongside of the terminology and arrangement to which exception has been taken there are many sections, even in the later chapters of *Sancta Sophia*, which are not open to any criticism; some of them, indeed, would seem from verbal resemblances, to be based directly upon St John of the Cross himself. In consequence, it would be easy to find passages supporting an entirely different theoretical position to that which has been criticized. Father Baker, in fact, in his teaching as in his own life, never reached (save possibly on his deathbed) the vision of peace, the goal of desire, from which he might survey and plot the route by which he had passed.

Whatever the explanation of his insufficiency, and whatever the extent of his aberrations, they must not be thought to destroy the excellence of Fr Baker's work. The science of souls and of mystical theology are both extremely difficult fields for the writers of guide-books, partly because both learning and experience are needed, partly because the very simplicity of pure spirituality and the unsearchability of the ways of God elude the theoretician. Even the very greatest— St Teresa, St John of the Cross themselves—are open to criticism on many points of arrangement or expression, whereas the writers of amiable platitudes or arid text-books can avoid all pitfalls and produce a work that never fired a soul with a single degree of charity. When all is said and done Fr Baker remains among the great, a "summity" as Abbot Cuthbert Butler would have said. When his book was first re-edited in its present form Bishop Hedley, who wrote on that occasion the most weighty appreciation of Fr Baker that has hitherto appeared,[32] remarked that the book was "a noviciate in itself". It is indeed a book of power for the noviciate and beyond, a book which will guide all for a part of their way, and may suffice to some for a very great part of their lives. But *nemo dat quod non habet*, and Fr Baker will not show a true contemplative the way to the summit. He may even mislead him into taking what is merely a foothill for the massif of Mount Carmel. Even prayer itself, considered as an endeavour or as a pursuit, may take the soul's eye off its one true mark. "God permits and wills that there should be one desire alone where He is, which is to keep the law of God perfectly, and to bear upon oneself the Cross of Christ."[33]

[32] "F. Baker's Sancta Sophia", in *Dublin Review*, October, 1876.
[33] *Ascent of Mount Carmel* I v (Peers I 33).

Chapter X

EPILOGUE

IN an earlier chapter of this book an attempt was made to give in outline the history of Christian mystical theology from early times until the fourteenth century. With Suso and Ruysbroeck the line of what may be called the medieval "doctors of mystical theology" came to an end. The Platonic current of spirituality of Nicholas of Cusa was not of the medieval world and in the event its influence was not lasting. On the other hand, the late fifteenth and still more the sixteenth century was a golden age of men and women, first in Italy and then far more abundantly in Spain, who were both eminent mystics and authoritative writers on the theory and practice of the mystical life, and in Spain between 1550 and 1650 there was a rich flowering of autobiographies, relations, directories and theological expositions of all kinds, among which the spiritual writings of St Teresa and St John of the Cross, and the theological treatises of John of St Thomas and Thomas of Valgornera were no more than peaks in a great range. In the seventeenth century French saints and spiritual writers took up the tale, with St Francis de Sales and Cardinal Bérulle and the other leaders of what Bremond has called the "invasion of the mystics", and it may in consequence be said that all subsequent writings on the mystical life in the Catholic Church have drawn inspiration from Spanish and French sources, among which the writings of the two great Carmelite saints have come to hold a place apart, confirmed and authorized as their teaching has been by the approval of the Church.

To all these saints and theologians the English medieval mystics were unknown, save in the narrow circle of the English Catholic recusants, whether at home or in exile. Historically speaking, they find their place in the stream of tradition between Eckhardt and Tauler and the great Spaniards, but the channel in which they lay was, so to speak, accidentally blocked by the isolation of England in the early fifteenth century and later by the Reformation, and the main river of tradition flowed from the Rhineland to the Spanish school by another and hitherto untraceable route. Yet though in fact the English stream was not destined to swell to a river the two writers of greatest influence, the author of *The Cloud* and Hilton, form a stage in the tradition which is not represented in any other country—the stage at which the strongly Neoplatonist doctrines of Eckhardt and Denis, partly reduced to traditional shape by Tauler and Thomas Gallus, were still further purified of their Neoplatonism and applied methodically and practically to the stages of the soul's progress as defined by the traditional spiritual teaching of the Church. In consequence, the two writers just mentioned stand midway between the unmethodical and uncoordinated teaching of the German mystics and the definitive system of theory and practice elaborated by the Spaniards, and if they had been more widely known in medieval Europe, or if England had remained in Catholic allegiance at the Reformation, they might well have had an important place in the direct succession of great masters.

Seen thus in retrospect, the so-called English mystics do not appear as a homogeneous group. Rolle, the earliest, is in part a representative of the traditional Augustinian, Victorine school and in part an individualist recording his own experiences. The author of *The Cloud* and Walter Hilton are indeed related to one another and have in common a basic theological position; they agree also in their criticism of

Rolle; but their aims and objects differ. Whereas *The Cloud* and *The Book* are directed to a small class and to a rare vocation, if not to a particular individual, Hilton comes nearest of the group to providing a complete guide to the spiritual life. Indeed, without either intending it or being aware of it, the author of *The Cloud* and Hilton were in fact the first writers in a modern European language to produce an example of kinds of writing that were to become extremely common: the instruction for a life of prayer and the guide to the stages of the spiritual life, each written in a direct, personal, non-technical style for all earnest readers who might wish to take the book up.

As for Julian of Norwich, she must stand as the principal English representative of a type of sanctity relatively common in Europe of the fourteenth century, that of the woman visionary or ecstatic who is also a guide and a prophet. She does not instruct methodically or explicitly; her strength lies in the impression she gives of having pondered the mysteries of the faith with spiritual eyes illuminated by contemplative grace; her effect upon us is to bear us away with her into a world that is wholly spiritual. She tells of what she has seen, and though she may give counsel and direction, she is not addressing a particular individual or class, but is putting into words, for all who have ears to hear, the inexpressible truth she has experienced. While it is clear that she is familiar with much of the literature of the contemplative life, including the writings of the two mystics we have just mentioned, the substance of her message comes from within, and from what she has seen in her soul.

In concluding this short sketch it may be of interest to summarize the mystical teaching of the two systematic writers, and compare with it the teaching of Father Baker in a later age. The author of *The Cloud* and Hilton are agreed that there is a specific difference between the knowledge and love of God possessed to a greater or less degree by all Christians of goodwill and the ineffable knowledge and love of the contemplative. Hilton in particular distinguishes them as the knowledge of faith and the knowledge of feeling, and by the last word he means, not the perception of the senses, the emotions or the mind, but the experience of the soul. They are in agreement, too, in regarding contemplative knowledge and love as wholly "infused", that is to say, they are the work of God within the soul to which the recipient contributes nothing but free consent, thus allowing a union between God and the soul. They are in consequence agreed that contemplation, like faith, is the pure gift of God and not a result of effort or merit, though they are clear that the degree of perfection attainable by the practice of the virtues and perseverance in prayer is a disposition normally found in those to whom God gives the further direct preparation for the contemplative graces. Yet on the other hand, they are agreed, at least by implication, that contemplation is a direct development, even though specifically distinct, of the sanctifying grace of the Christian life first bestowed at baptism, and they would have accepted the untheological but descriptively apt Teresan metaphor of the chrysalis and the butterfly. Neither of them directly faces and answers the question, which would seem to arise inevitably, whether all devout Christians may aspire, and hope to receive enablement, to attain to the mystical life. On the other hand, there are occasional traces of the opinion, half Neoplatonic, half based on Aristotelian categories of thought, that all grace is as a "form" coming upon the soul, and when the disposition is perfect, the form supervenes. On the other hand there is the explicit assertion that contemplation is the free gift of God, and that the relevant instructions are given to be used only by those convinced in one way or another of their call.

Of the two writers, the author of *The Cloud* excels in the

clear instructions and fine analysis of the initial stages of contemplative prayer, while Hilton's strength lies in his distinction of the active and contemplative lives and his fuller
description of the stages. Neither dwells in any detail on the
highest degrees of the contemplative life as given by Ruysbroeck, St Teresa, St John of the Cross and others, and whereas with the writers just mentioned there is abundant evidence,
external and internal, that they themselves have directly
experienced the sublime states they describe, there is no external and little internal evidence in the case of the two
Englishmen. Most readers will feel assured that they were in
fact contemplatives, but they will probably feel also that their
range was far smaller than that of Ruysbroeck and the great
Spaniards.

The opinion has been expressed in the past that Father
Baker's teaching is a prolongation of that of *The Cloud* and
Hilton, but a careful reading of his works does not fully bear
this out. Father Baker certainly sought out the English
medieval writers and recommended them to those whom he
directed and, through those, to all "discreet, well-minded"
souls, and in this sense he may be said to have revived their
teaching and influence. He also wrote a valuable and sympathetic commentary on *The Cloud*; he gave the work to his
nuns as a *vade mecum* and seems to have regarded himself as a
follower of the unknown mystic's instructions. Yet in his
classical work, *Sancta Sophia*, he is, as has been seen, extremely
eclectic. Many other writers, not all of the same school, are
recommended and his system, so far as it is logical and complete, rests chiefly upon the spiritual writers of the Counter-
Reformation, and contains many parts and elements not
treated explicitly by the medieval writers. Moreover, the two
most valuable single elements in his scheme, the prayer of acts
of the will and the teaching on inspirations, are largely his
own contribution and owe nothing directly to the medieval

mystics. While, therefore, Father Baker had an essential part in the preservation and presentation of the works of the medieval writers, and while we may even say that without his interest and industry the rediscovery of them might have been long delayed, and perhaps not fully completed till our own day, he cannot be regarded as standing to them as a disciple or a continuator. It might even be argued that he failed to grasp some of the main principles of mystical theology that they had grasped, even while he contributed teaching of his own that was to be of the greatest practical value.

Finally, we may say that the English mystics, however regarded, and whatever may have been their shortcomings and obscurities, form a group which, for the force and purity of their traditional doctrine, and for the unusual attractions both of their personalities and of their style of writing, is unequalled by any other single regional or national group in the later medieval world. After six centuries they still retain their power to attract and to guide those able and willing to follow their teaching.

INDEX